Theological Themes
of the Old Testament

Theological Themes
of the Old Testament

Creation, Covenant, Cultus, and Character

MARTY E. STEVENS

CASCADE *Books* · Eugene, Oregon

THEOLOGICAL THEMES OF THE OLD TESTAMENT
Creation, Covenant, Cultus, and Character

Cascade Books
An Imprint of Wipf and Stock Publishers
199 W. 8th Ave., Suite 3
Eugene, OR 97401

www.wipfandstock.com

ISBN 13: 978-1-60608-816-6

Cataloging-in-Publication data:

Stevens, Marty E., 1953–

    Theological themes of the Old Testament : creation, covenant,
cultus, and character / Marty E. Stevens.

    xii + 172 p. ; cm. 23 — Includes bibliographical references and
index.

    ISBN 13: 978-1-60608-816-6

    1. Creation—Biblical teaching. 2. Covenant theology. 3. Worship in
the Bible. 4. Ethics in the Bible. I. Title.

BS1199 .C6 S84 2010

Manufactured in the U.S.A.

Contents

Preface

THE OLD TESTAMENT IS an ancient collection of theological reflections on life with God that the church has claimed as authoritative Scripture. Most of us become acquainted with the Old Testament by reading selected passages in worship services, learning certain stories in Sunday school, or reading brief devotional texts. Some of us have read books or sections of the Old Testament in an effort to become more familiar with its content. Introductory courses on the Old Testament typically march through the canon chronologically from Genesis to Malachi, highlighting key characters and events along the way. This book, however, engages the Old Testament thematically rather than canonically. I have selected four themes that permeate the texts of the Old Testament, and I seek to locate those themes longitudinally throughout the canon. Granted, certain themes are the particular focus of certain Old Testament books. But all the themes occur across the breadth of the Old Testament canon and, for that matter, across other ancient Near Eastern cultures.

The first chapter starts at the beginning of the Old Testament with the theme of *creation*. Focused at first in the early chapters of Genesis, we see a God who is in relationship with creation from the very beginning. The theme of creation is explored in other books under the rubrics "creation in the meantime" and "creation in the end times." God uses elements of creation to provide for and punish humans, and eventually to bring about new life.

The second chapter addresses the theme of *covenant*, the binding alliance between God and Israel. The sociohistorical background for covenants in the ancient Near East is explored, leading to examination of several covenants described in the Old Testament, including the covenants with Noah, Abraham, Israel at Sinai, and David.

The third theme is *cultus*, the academic term for worship rituals. Addressing probably the most misunderstood aspect of the Old Testament, the third chapter explains the cultic structures and rituals that provided people with access to the divine presence. Many texts address the vital issue of God's dwelling with the people, and their grateful response to God's choice of Israel as a holy nation.

The final chapter addresses the theme of *character*, by which I mean the moral fiber of the individual and the community. By examining Old Testament texts across the canon, but especially the Wisdom literature, we can glean what attributes and behaviors are nurtured or discouraged.

The intended audience for this book is laypeople who want to know more about the Old Testament, whether in personal study, church groups, college classrooms, or seminary courses. Accordingly, I have deliberately avoided dense, academic language. Footnotes are not provided because the information presented here is either well known in scholarly circles or the product of my own scholarship. Those interested in further reading on each theme will find suggestions at the end.

The ancient texts are taken seriously enough not to be taken literally. That is, I understand the Old Testament texts to be *theological* texts first and foremost, not texts that Westerners would label as history or science. Throughout the chapters, I distinguish between the world of the narrative (that is, what the story wants readers to think) and the world of the author (that is, the historical or social circumstances of the author). Holding these together in creative tension allows modern readers to step into the ancient texts and learn something about who God is and who we are.

Acknowledgments

"NECESSITY IS THE MOTHER of invention." This book arose from my need to find a textbook for an intensive class I was scheduled to teach in January-term 2009 at the Lutheran Theological Seminary at Gettysburg. Thirty-three students had registered for the course "Theological Themes of the Old Testament," and I could not locate an appropriate textbook. I was wandering the Wipf and Stock Publishers book exhibit at the Society of Biblical Literature meeting in November 2008 when K. C. Hanson casually asked, "May I help you?" After I had vented my angst over not having found a suitable textbook for the Old Testament course, K. C. inquired, "Would you like to write that book?" Thanks, K. C., for being this book's midwife.

My January class was the Petri dish for the development of these four theological themes, including through helpful comments on a draft manuscript from student Linda N. Smith. My friend Timothy E. Braband read a draft and provided the perspective of a smart person of faith. Dean Robin J. Steinke, the faculty, and the staff at Gettysburg Seminary continue to provide a place for me to flourish. My mother, Ruby M. Stevens, provides support and encouragement in ways that only a mother can. Thanks to you all.

ONE

Creation

WITH THE OPENING WORDS of the Bible, we are witnesses to creation. Painted in broad strokes in the first two chapters of Genesis, the depth and breadth of God's creative genius is recalled by ancient Israelites, intentionally inviting all future generations of readers to be attentive to the theme of creation throughout the following books. Biblical insights regarding the beginning of the universe and its inhabitants will begin this chapter. Then we turn to the biblical witness of how God harnesses creation for providence and punishment; we examine ways in which elements of creation sustain and destroy. Finally, we explore the hopeful vision of renewed creation articulated in the Old Testament.

CREATION IN THE BEGINNING

The broad outline of the first chapter of Genesis is familiar to anyone with minimal exposure to the Old Testament: creation of the universe, plants, animals, and humans; God's speaking creation into existence; seven days; the words "it was good." The second chapter of Genesis, then, further describes the creation of Adam and Eve in the Garden of Eden. A close reading of these two chapters reveals the differences between them; these differences result in the first two chapters generally being attributed to different authorial sources.

Genesis 1:1—2:4a

The literary structure of the text demonstrates its deliberate crafting as a liturgy of praise. In this regard, we note the use of the number seven—a number that represented completeness in the ancient world. Creation is completed in seven days, represented literarily by seven paragraphs in the Hebrew text. Important words are used in multiples of seven: "good" (seven times) "earth" (twenty-one times), and "God" (thirty-five times). Verse 1 has seven words in Hebrew:

1. *in-beginning*

2. *created*

3. *God*

4. direct-object marker

5. *the-heavens*

6. *and* plus direct-object marker

7. *the-earth.*

Verse 2, using fourteen Hebrew words, describes the earth as "formless" (*tohu*) and "void" (*bohu*). The words *tohu* and *bohu* provide the overarching structure for the first six days of creation. "Formless" means "without any structure," but the first three days establish the structure of the heavens and the earth. "Void" means "without any content," but the second set of three days fills in the structure with content. Parallels can be noted between days 1 and 4, days 2 and 5, and days 3 and 6. If one imagines the white space on this page as *tohu* and *bohu* (the "formless and void"), space is structured by the bold lines, and filled with content by the italicized words, as depicted in figure 1:

FIGURE 1

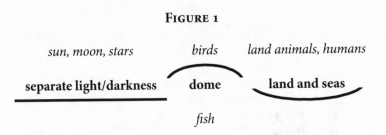

The literary symmetry of Gen 1:1—2:4a, the so-called First Creation Narrative, can also be illustrated by lining up the parallel days in two columns as in figure 2. The climax is not the creation of humanity, as is often asserted, but rather the creation of the Sabbath on day seven. In this creation drama, God speaks the elements of creation into existence. Perhaps we imagine a powerful deity with a magisterial, sonorous voice, whose creative commands reverberate throughout the cosmos. In the biblical text, each day's narrative begins with "and God said." This is the normal, everyday Hebrew word for "said"—there is no *special* speaking by God, no magical use of the divine voice that is not also an attribute of the human voice. Moreover, what God says is grammatically not a command but rather an invitation or supplication. A command is second-person direct address: "Read this book! Students, put down your pencils!" A command to create light would be something like, "Light, appear!" But what God says in Gen 1:3 is not addressed to the light directly, as a command. Rather, the

FIGURE 2

DAY 0 (1:1–2)
Setting the scene at the beginning: "The earth was

WITHOUT STRUCTURE   WITHOUT CONTENT
(tohu)   *(bohu)*

and darkness covered the face of the deep,
while a wind from God swept over the face of the waters."

DAY 1 (1:3–5)	DAY 4 (1:14–19)
A. Light/Darkness	A. Lights
B. Named "Day"/"Night"	B. Task: Govern and separate
DAY 2 (1:6–8)	DAY 5 (1:20–23)
A. Dome with waters above and below	A. Aquatic and aerial animals
B. Named "Sky"	B. Blessing: Fill water and sky
DAY 3 (1:9–13)	DAY 6 (1:24–31)
A. Gathered waters and dry land	A. Land animals and humans
B. Named "Seas"/ "Earth"	B. Blessing: Fill land and govern
C. Vegetation	C. Task: Provide food

DAY 7 (2:1–3)
A. Heavens and earth finished
B. Cessation and consecration of Sabbath

grammar is invitation, supplication, petition, and wish—
something like, "May light happen," addressed to a third
party: probably the formless void. Similarly, on day 2 God
petitions, "Let there be a dome [may a dome happen] in
the midst of the waters, and let [may] it separate the waters
from the waters" (1:6). Interestingly, immediately after this
petition, the narrator tells us, "So God made the dome."
Day 3 begins with God's supplication, "Let [May] the waters under the sky be gathered together into one place,
and let [may] the dry land appear" (1:9). After God names
"Seas" and "Earth," the language of invitation becomes
more explicit when God does not command vegetation
to appear or command the earth to provide vegetation.
Rather God says, "Let [May] the earth put forth vegetation" (1:11). The earth is portrayed as an essential partner,
one who is invited to participate in the creative venture.
One wonders what would have happened if the earth self-
ishly remarked, "No. I don't want to put forth vegetation."
But any suspense aroused by the invitatory language is
resolved quickly in the next verse when "the earth brought
forth vegetation." And so the structure of the heavens and
earth is formed.

When we move to the right half of the creation chart
(the filling of the heavens and earth with content), the
supplication language of each day is supplemented with
explicit language of God's own creative work. Suspense
inherent in the language of petition is immediately resolved by the narrator's explicit claims of God's personal
intervention. On day 4, God says," Let there be lights [May
lights happen]" (1:14), and the narrator describes, "God
made the two great lights" (1:15). Creative activity on day
5 involves the active participation of the waters, since God
says, "Let [May] the waters bring forth swarms of living

creatures, and let [may] birds fly above the earth across the dome of the sky" (1:20). Then the narrator clarifies, "So God created" the aquatic and aerial animals. Day 6 parallels the previous day, when God says, "Let [May] the earth bring forth living creatures" (1:24), and the narrator clarifies, "God made" the earthbound animals. Creation of humanity also follows this double pattern of divine invitation and creation. God says, "Let us [May we] make humankind" (1:26), and the narrator's notice follows: "God created humankind." The importance of the creation of humanity is emphasized by the literary construction of a three-part parallel poem:

A	B	C	D
And-[he]-created	God	humanity	in-his-image

D′	B	A	C′
In-the-likeness-of	God	he-created	them

D″	A	C′	
Male-and-female	[he]-created	them	

Notice the poetic progressive parallelism of the element labeled with the letter D. The vaguer "in his image" is further described as "in the likeness of" and then clarified as "male and female." Day 7 contains no divine speech at all; we rely on the trustworthy narrator to describe the conclusion to this grand endeavor.

Modern readers are struck by the incongruence of the plural pronoun in this part of the text (1:26). For ancients, "we/us" referred to the divine council in heaven. Just as earthly kings have a council of advisors, the divine King has a divine council—heavenly beings who may be consulted on upcoming actions. Psalm 82:1 specifically mentions the divine council; the prose setting of Job presumes such a body (Job 1:6–12 and 2:1–6). Other explanations for the use of plural here include an appearance by the Christian Trinity, the appearance of Lady Wisdom (Prov 8:22–31), or the presence of a divine female consort.

Having noted the careful literary construction of Gen 1:1—2:4a, we turn to the questions of authorship and purpose. Scholars agree that this text resulted from theological reflections of priests and other elites during their time of exile in Babylon, beginning in 587 BCE. Several clues in the text support this assertion. First, the text is constructed as a liturgy, with refrains providing summary and punctuation to the text. The refrain, "And it was evening and it was morning, the *n*th day," marks the sequential passing of creative time. Second, God evaluates the creative efforts as "good" or "very good." In ancient Israel the priests were the arbiters of what was "good," be it a sacrificial animal or human behavior. Third, the verb "separate" occurs on days 1, 2, and 4 as an integral purpose of the lights and the dome. The priests were the functionaries in ancient Israel responsible for maintaining separation between the clean and the unclean, the holy and the profane (see chapter 3, below). The word *separate* as adjective and as verb is also used frequently to describe Israel's unique stance among the nations: "You shall be holy to me; for I the Lord am holy, and I have separated you from the other peoples to be mine" (Lev 20:26). Included on day 6 are instructions about appropriate food for humanity, also a central concern of the priests. Fourth, language of blessing and consecration (activities associated with priestly rituals) permeate days 4, 5, and 6. Finally, the climax of creation in the Sabbath rest is of central concern to the priests.

We should not be surprised that theological reflections by priests on the beginnings of the universe would include confirmation of goodness, clarity of roles and duties, and Sabbath. In exile in Babylon, the priests reconstructed recollections of God's creative activity in ways that would reinforced their own pivotal role in Israelite society once the exile ended. Understanding Sabbath as built into the rhythms of the universe inspires confidence in the God who can afford to take a day off. When the surrounding Babylonian culture interpreted the exile as the defeat of the God of Israel by the God of Babylon, this text celebrates the powerful yet noncoercive Creator of all things. That is, the construction of the narrative is hopeful in and of itself, anticipating the release of the exiles by a good and gracious God who will then restore Israel to its unique role among the nations.

The description of vegetation and animal life in this chapter is effusive. After concise, spare language on days 1 and 2, the narrator suddenly engages in extreme verbosity to describe the diversity of plant and animal life created in the next two days. In day 3, "the earth brought forth vegetation: plants yielding seed of every kind, and trees of every kind bearing fruit with the seed in it" (1:12). This is noticeably different from the simple sentences on the previous two days. On day 5, "God created the great sea monsters and every living creature that moves, of every kind, with which the waters swarm, and every winged bird of every kind" (1:21). On day 6, "God made the wild animals of the earth of every kind, and the cattle of every kind, and

everything that creeps upon the ground of every kind"
(1:25). God then commissions humanity to rule "over the
fish of the sea, and over the birds of the air, and over the
cattle, and over all the wild animals of the earth, and over
every creeping thing that creeps upon the earth" (1:26).
Why would the authors use such detailed and convoluted
descriptions of plant and animal species when clearly a
more sparse description would have sufficed? Such ef-
fusiveness underscores the all-encompassing nature of
this Creator God, who is concerned with the ordering of
the vegetation, fruit trees, sea creatures, birds, cattle, and
creeping things. We may also detect an allusion to a royal
custom in the ancient Near East of planting botanical
gardens and populating zoos as a sign of luxury, wealth,
and control over the countries of origin. When the king
enjoyed his garden filled with cedars transplanted from
Lebanon and with balsam from the Dead Sea shores, he
could symbolically savor his sovereignty over the peoples
of those regions. As the final editors of all the traditions
that came together into the Pentateuch (the first five books
of the Bible), the Priestly source placed their reflections on
creation at the beginning of the entire narrative of Israel's
life with God. Indeed, the beginning is a very good place
to start since the beginning of any text influences reading
strategies throughout the text.

At this point we may profitably inquire about the
division of creation narratives in the middle of v. 4 in
chapter 2 rather than at the end of chapter 1, for example.
(Chapter numbers were inserted in the Middle Ages.) The
reason for the division is twofold. First, the coordinating
conjunction "thus" in 2:1 connects the opening verses in
chapter 2 to the final verses in chapter 1. The conjunction

"thus" is appropriate since chapter 1 as well as verses 1–3 of chapter 2 are intimately related to one another in content. Second, the Hebrew word *toledot*, meaning "generations" or "lineages" marks the first part of v. 4 (called 4a). Here the *toledot* statement ends the Priestly narrative; elsewhere in Genesis, the Priestly writers use the *toledot* statement to begin the next section of narrative. Ten *toledot* statements are found in Genesis, and they serve to structure the overall narrative by delineating the familial story of one or more of the key persons. Locations of the remaining nine *toledot* statements and their familial interests introduced by the statements are

- Gen 5:1   Adam
- Gen 6:9   Noah
- Gen 10:1   Noah's sons
- Gen 11:10   Shem (ancestor of the Semites)
- Gen 11:27   Terah (not Abraham, as would be expected)
- Gen 25:12   Ishmael
- Gen 25:19   Isaac
- Gen 36:1   Esau/Edom
- Gen 37:2   Jacob

Genesis 2:4b–25

With the second half of verse 4 (called 4b), we begin another account of the beginnings of the heavens and earth. Careful readers will immediately note the use of "the LORD God" as the name of the Creator in chapter 2 (versus "God" in chapter 1). English translations use "the LORD" (all capital letters) to signal the underlying Hebrew word YHWH, the personal divine name revealed to Moses at Mount Sinai (Exod 3:14). Technically speaking, the use of this personal name in texts placed prior to Exodus 3 is an anachronism—that is, a reference in the wrong time period. (One who might describe the biblical Abraham as talking on a cell phone uses an anachronism, for instance.) Since the name YHWH had not yet been revealed, how could the implied narrator in Genesis 2 know it? Scholars surmise that the author is writing in a time post-Exodus, knows the name, and simply uses it in his text. The narrative in chapter 2 lacks the systematic structure apparent in chapter 1. The author does not seem to be concerned with the creation of the heavens and the earth per se, but with the inhabitants of the earth; it is as though the writer of chapter 2 has picked up the narrative in day 6 of chapter 1. But this is not entirely accurate, since in this story, the human is created first, before any vegetation or animals. Vegetation is apparently not growing because (1) there was no rain yet, and (2) there was no human farmer for it yet. In place of rain, however, a mist provided life-giving water.

Recall the lofty, poetic language of the creation of humanity in Genesis 1 and compare the sparse description here: "Then the LORD God formed man [human] from the dust of the ground and breathed into his nostrils the breath of life; and the man [human] became a living being" (2:7). The verb "formed" used here is not the same word as the verbs used in chapter 1 ("created" or "made"). This verb is much more hands-on: a potter *forms* a vessel out of clay (for example, in 2 Sam 17:28; Isa 29:16; Jer 18:4–6), a carver forms wood into a graven image (Isa 44:9–12; Hab 2:18). This story tells of soil watered by mist, so the image here is of God making mud pies! What God forms is *'adam*, a Hebrew word that can be translated "human," "humanity," or "Adam." (Many English translations use the word *man* here. The specific Hebrew word [*'ish*] for the English word "man," will show up in Gen 2:23.) Hebrew presents a word-play here, since *'adam* is formed from the ground or soil (*'adamah*). Capturing the word-play in English would require a translation like "earthling from the earth" or "human from the humus" or, to use a proper name, "Dusty from the dust" or "Sollie from the soil." This mud pie become upright is not yet a living being; it will take the inspiration of the divine breath to bring about that miracle. Again, notice the intimate image of the deity presented here: the divine hands get dirty, and divine breath goes from mouth to mouth, or from mouth to nose.

Only after this mud pie comes to life does the LORD God plant a garden and set the *'adam* in it. To create the garden, God does not involve the earth in bringing forth vegetation as in the previous chapter. Here, God digs in the soil and plants a garden, growing "every tree that is pleasant to the sight and good for food" (2:9). Hence the garden is a "garden of delight" (Hebrew: *'eden*). (When the Hebrew Scriptures were translated into Greek in the third century BCE, the Greek word used for Hebrew *'eden* was *paradeison*, source of the English word "paradise.") The narrative sequence is interrupted for four verses to describe the garden of delight as the source of four major waterways in the ancient world. Obscure to modern readers, this narrative aside situates the garden of delight in the center of the known universe and confirms its life-giving powers. When the story resumes, we learn that the *'adam* is put in the garden "to till it and keep it" (2:15). The core meaning of the first Hebrew verb here is "serve"; depending on what or whom is being served, various English verbs may be used. Many English versions translate the word as "till," since the ground is the object of service. When God is the object of service, we find verbs like "worship" (Exod 3:12) or "serve" (Josh 24:15). Recalling the core meaning of "serve" reminds us of humanity's intimate connection to the land and of our responsibility for it. Here in the garden of delight the *'adam* is given the first divine permission, conditioned with a prohibition. With the extravagant abundance of vegetation still reverberating from chapter 1, readers are inclined first of all to delight in the permission granted to feast on "every tree of the garden"; the prohibition from one tree seems inconsequential.

The next verse poses a striking contrast to the abundance of all of chapter 1 and of chapter 2 so far. Conditioned by the sevenfold refrain of "it was good" in chapter 1, readers are now taken aback by the divine pronouncement "It is not good" (2:18). In response to the lack of partnership, "out of the ground the LORD God formed every animal of the field and every bird of the air" (2:19). With naming rights given to the *'adam*, the LORD God waits anxiously for one whom the *'adam* would name "Helper." When no such partner is found, the LORD God goes to plan B, making a Helper from the very substance of the *'adam*, no doubt confident that such a one would satisfy the need. Consistent with making mudpies, the LORD God gets the divine hands dirty again by performing surgery on the *'adam*. The Hebrew word-play emphasizes the fitness of the Helper. This time, the LORD God makes the *'ish* from the *'ishah*. English captures this wordplay with "woman" from "man." This narrative as a whole has a completely different feel from chapter 1. Here, the LORD God is an intimate friend, is adaptable, and is willing to get down and dirty. Water is an important concern, whether in the form of rain, mist, or four rivers. The text reads more like a story and less like a liturgy.

For these reasons and others, scholars posit that this text resulted from theological reflections of southern Israelites living in the land of Canaan. Called the Yahwist-source or the J-source (from the German spelling that begins with *J*), narratives from this source may have been written as early as the reign of Solomon in the first quarter of the tenth century BCE (although scholars debate this). As subsistence farmers and nomadic herders, the southern Israelites were intrinsically connected to the soil, depending on rainfall to nourish plants and animals. The ability Israel's God to provide water is of critical importance. The other peoples of Canaan believed that Ba'al was the god who controlled water, and thus controlled fertility. This text presents an outright refutation of the Canaanite god's claim to preeminence.

Other Ancient Near Eastern Creation Narratives

Here we broaden the conversation to include two narratives of ancient Mesopotamia from the first half of the second millennium BCE. The best known is called *Enuma Elish*, from its first two words. In this account, an epic battle takes place between two deities: Marduk, the god of wind and storm, and Tiamat, the goddess of the sea and chaos. At a point in the battle when Tiamat opens her mouth, Marduk fills her full of air and then kills her with an arrow. Dividing her corpse in half lengthwise, he creates the sky out of the upper half and the earth out of the lower half; her spittle is used to create rain, her eyes give rise to the great Tigris and Euphrates Rivers, and her breasts form the mountains. Marduk proposes to the other (junior) gods that a new race be created to take over the work of providing for their needs. To that end, Tiamat's widower and commander-in-chief, Kingu, is put to death, so that his blood can be used to form humanity. The gods live happily ever after, relaxing while humanity performs their drudgery.

The Epic of Athrahasis sounds a somewhat similar theme. Three chief gods apportion the universe among themselves (heavens, water, and earth), and junior gods are put to work providing necessary food and drink. Soon the junior gods rebel, complaining of their arduous labor. The chief gods agree to create a new race to take on the laborious work. To provide raw material for the new creatures, the leader of the rebellion is killed, and his blood is mixed with clay, upon which all the gods spit. Specially appointed birth goddesses pinch off portions of the blood, clay, and spittle mixture; shape them; and keep them for nine months, after which time the human race emerges. The noise of humanity disturbs the deities' rest, however, and eventually enrages the gods. The gods reduce the human population by sending a devastating flood, which Athrahasis, his family, and pairs of animals survive by means of a boat.

Common throughout the ancient Near East was the motif of *Chaoskampf*: creation out of primordial conflict. By contrast, the creation accounts in Genesis present the

God of Israel's creative efforts as without conflict. The elements are there: the heavens, the earth, the sea/deep (Greek *abyss*), and sea monsters, but they are not representatives of deities fighting with one another for supremacy. Water is often a veiled reference to chaos in the Old Testament, but in Genesis 1 a wind from God is sweeping over the waters, obviously controlling them. Humanity is not created from the blood of a conquered or rebellious god to serve the capricious needs of gods living in luxury. There are hints in biblical texts other than Genesis, however, of the common motif of *Chaoskampf* lurking underneath the surface. Several texts give witness to God's conflict with sea monsters named Leviathan or Rahab: "You broke the heads of the dragons in the waters. You crushed the heads of Leviathan" (Ps 74:13b–14a); "You crushed Rahab like a carcass" (Ps 89:10a); "Can you draw out Leviathan with a fishhook, or press down its tongue with a cord? Can you put rope in its nose, or pierce its jaw with a hook? . . . Will you play with it as with a bird, or will you put it on leash for your girls" (Job 41:1–2, 5)? "Was it not you who cut Rahab into pieces, who pierced the dragon" (Isa 51:9b)? These texts show that the surrounding ancient Near Eastern cultures influenced ancient Israelite thought more than a simple reading of Genesis would imply.

Creation Outside of Genesis

Surprisingly, theological reflection on the beginning of the universe is not widespread in the Old Testament. Two psalms explicitly celebrate the beginnings of the world. Psalm 8 marvels at the dignity and honor bestowed on humanity when considered against the vast backdrop of the cosmos. Any of us who have looked into the night sky could wonder with the psalmist, "When I look at your heavens, the works of your fingers, the moon and the stars that you have established, what are human beings that you are mindful of them, and mortals that you care for them" (Ps 8:3–4)? The longer Psalm 104 rehearses the creation of heavens (vv. 2–3); earth (v. 4); waters (vv. 5–13); vegetation and landscape features (vv. 14–18); and celestial bodies, darkness, and light (vv. 19–23). In this poem, the psalmist stresses the orderliness of creation: springs are to quench the thirst of animals, grass is for beasts, cedars are for the birds' nests, fir trees are for the storks, darkness is for the nocturnal animals of the forest, and daylight is for human productivity.

The other extended creation narrative outside Genesis is Job 38–42. After refusing to recognize his affliction as justifiable, Job is finally silenced when God speaks from a whirlwind. God's extended speech addresses the creation of a wide variety of elements, including the heavens, the earth, the sea, water in all its forms (rain, snow, ice, hail, etc.), light and darkness, and beasts. Most scholars interpret the divine speech as essentially saying to Job, "Who are you to question me, the Creator of the world?" While it certainly has that effect, another purpose may be to sketch the breadth of the diverse creation. Job argues against the narrow mindedness of the "orthodox" notion of suffering as retribution; God's speech argues against the narrow-minded notion of the orders of creation, subtly expanding the Israelite notion of what is "meant to be." The divine speech from the whirlwind takes creative credit for creation in all of its wildness and unpredictability.

CREATION IN THE MEANTIME

God is convincingly portrayed as the Creator of the cosmos and its inhabitants in Genesis 1–2. But God does not cease being Creator in Genesis 3, as if God's creative work is finished once the cosmic elements are set in place and all the flora and fauna are initially generated. The biblical witness is that God is Creator not only at the beginning of things but throughout history and even beyond. In this section, we will explore some key biblical passages related to what has been called "continuing creation" or "sustaining creation." Specifically, we will note how God employs creation for human providence, and how God uses creation for human punishment. With words like "employ" or "use," we do not mean to imply a strictly instrumental use of the elements of creation. The above discussion of the supplication language in Genesis 1 negates any such understanding of the creative elements as instrumental for the sole benefit of humans. God invites elements of creation to participate in bringing forth new life in its immense diversity. God blessed the flying creatures and the swimming creatures before humanity was introduced into the mix. Nevertheless, as Creator, the biblical God "uses" creation for and against humanity, sometimes with consequences far beyond the immediate audience.

Providence

By using the word *providence*, we mean to point to the ongoing divine activity of *providing* for humanity by means of the physical creation. The theological doctrinal use of the word to indicate divine foreknowledge or plan is explicitly not in view here. In the previous section, Psalm

104 was cited as expressing concern with the beginnings of the universe, including with the orderliness of creation. Here we note again the beneficial purpose of elements of creation: "You cause the grass to grow for the cattle, and plants for people to use, to bring forth food from the earth, and wine to gladden the human heart, oil to make the face shine, and bread to strengthen the human heart" (Ps 104:14–15). After noting the sheltering places for birds and land animals in various trees and locales, the psalmist summarizes divine providence for all life: "These all look to you to give them their food in due season; when you give it to them, they gather it up; when you open your hand, they are filled with good things. When you hide your face, they are dismayed; when you take away their breath, they die and return to their dust. When you send forth your spirit [breath], they are created; and you renew the face of the ground" (Ps 104:27–30). The psalmist explicitly credits God with life-sustaining providence.

PROVIDENCE IN PROCREATION

The first example of God's ongoing providence for humanity is in the natural processes of procreation, propagation, and reproduction in the plant and animal kingdoms. Already in the first verses of Genesis, the ability to "be fruitful and multiply" is part of the fabric of the universe. We noted the excessive, convoluted language in Genesis 1 that specifies "plants yielding seed of every kind, and trees of every kind bearing fruit with the seed in it" (1:12) and "the great sea monsters and every living creature that moves, of every kind, with which the waters swarm, and every winged bird of every kind" (1:21) and "the wild animals of the earth of every kind, and the cattle of every kind, and everything that creeps upon the ground of every kind" (1:25). That is, "fruit/seed" is used nine times, and "of every kind" is used ten times in a short span of verses to describe God's creative activity related to plants and animals. God's blessings of animals and humans on Days 5 and 6 are the same: "Be fruitful and multiply" (1:22, 28). Further, God announces the gift of food for animals and humans: "See, I have given you every plant yielding seed that is upon the face of all the earth, and every tree with seed in its fruit; you shall have them for food" (1:29). What else can this mean except that the means to reproduce new plants and animals is hard-wired into creation? Diverse vegetation has been created with the means provided to produce more vegetation. Aquatic, aerial, and land animals, including humans, have the means to procreate so that they "fruit" new animals and become numerous. Readers are meant to understand that fertility of plants and animals is the consequence of divine blessing.

Providence in Abundance of the Land

Carrying out the divine blessing to "be fruitful and multiply" leads to abundance in the land. The stock phrase in the Old Testament for this abundance is "a land flowing with milk and honey," a phrase that occurs eighteen times, all but five times in the Pentateuch. The first instance of the phrase, in Exod 3:8, further identifies the land as "good and broad." Deut 8:7–10 paints a picture of abundance for the Israelites poised on the edge of the land: "For the LORD your God is bringing you into a good land, a land with flowing streams, with springs and underground waters welling up in valleys and hills, a land of wheat and barley, of vines and fig trees and pomegranates, a land of olive trees and honey, a land where you may eat bread without scarcity, where you will lack nothing, a land whose stones are iron and from whose hills you may mine copper. You shall eat your fill and bless the LORD your God for the good land that he has given you."

The statutes and ordinances in Exodus, Leviticus, and Deuteronomy may be considered indications of God's providence. Clearly the laws are written for a settled community engaged in agriculture and herding, and scholars suspect the laws were written down long after the chronology presented in the Pentateuch. For example, "When fire breaks out and catches in thorns so that the stacked grain or the standing grain or the field is consumed, the one who started the fire shall make full restitution" (Exod 22:6); "You shall not delay to make offerings from the fullness of your harvest and from the outflow of your presses" (Exod 22:29). In their present literary setting, presented to the people in the wilderness, the regulations presuppose abundant harvests and plentiful herds, and serve to reinforce God's initiative to lead the people to a promised land. In fact, we may assert that the extended instructions regarding appropriate offerings, sacrificial and otherwise, may be understood as signs of God's abundant providence in the land. Finally, we may mention the Sabbatical and Jubilee years as described in Leviticus 25 as evidence of God's providence in the land. In the seventh (Sabbatical) and fiftieth (Jubilee) years, the land was to lie fallow for its own sabbatical rest. Whether the Sabbatical year or Jubilee year was ever enacted as prescribed is immaterial to the theological point made in the text, which is that God will provide abundantly from creation for those who trust and obey: "The land will yield its fruit, and you will eat your fill and live on it securely. Should you ask, What shall we eat in the seventh year, if we may not sow or gather in our crop? I will order my blessing for you in the sixth year, so that it will yield a crop for three years" (Lev 25:19–21).

Providence in the Wilderness

Before entering this promised land of milk and honey, the Israelites experience God's providence in the wilderness (Hebrew: *midbar*). In the Pentateuch, the reference is to the geographic area between Egypt and the Dead Sea, an area labeled on Bible maps as Sinai or Negeb/Negev, with specific territories like the Wilderness of Zin, the Wilderness of Paran, and the like. The *midbar* is an area of extreme aridity, with rocky hills where only scrub bushes cling to life. The small valleys between the hills create natural channels called *wadis* for the occasional rains. Natural springs create oases where life may flourish.

The wilderness traditions in the Old Testament are predominantly found in Exodus 16–18 and Numbers 11–21, the chapters bracketing the Israelite encampment at Mount Sinai. In these traditional stories, the people murmur in the *midbar* about some perceived lack, which God then remedies, often through the intercession or agency of Moses. Not surprisingly, water and food are issues of utmost concern in these traditions. The lack of potable water is the focus of Exod 15:22–25 and 17:1–7. In the earlier tradition, bitter water is made sweet when a tree is thrown into the pool. In the later tradition, water flows from the rocky side of a mountain when Moses strikes it with his rod. In between these bookends is the tradition about the lack of suitable food. In Exod 16:3 the Israelites recall (incorrectly) their life in Egypt "when we sat by the fleshpots and ate our fill of bread." (Are these the same folks as those who made bricks without straw?) The divine response doubly addresses the lack of food: "At twilight you shall eat meat, and in the morning you shall have your fill of bread" (Exod 16:12). A covey of quails covering the camp at twilight and manna covering the ground in the morning demonstrate God's ability to provide sustenance even in desperate geography. On the other side of the yearlong stay at Mount Sinai, the people's trek in the *midbar* again causes them to murmur about the lack of suitable food. Readers probably sympathize with their murmurings about the monotonous manna; what doesn't evoke such sympathy is their (incorrect) recollection of their life in Egypt: "If only we had meat to eat! We remember the fish we used to eat in Egypt for nothing, the cucumbers, the melons, the leeks, the onions, and the garlic" (Num 11:4b–5). (Making bricks without straw under the Egyptian sun was "for nothing"?) This time God does not address their complaint for twenty-five verses; the suspense builds as to whether their request will be granted. The narrator reports that God does send quail meat for them to eat: "a day's journey on this side and a day's journey on the other side, all around the camp, about two cubits [three feet] deep on the ground" (Num 11:31) so that the people have to work thirty-six hours straight to collect all the quail. This story teaches that God provides, with an exclamation point!

Punishment

Even as the Bible describes creation as an instrument God uses to provide for humans, the Bible also describes God's use of creation as punishment for human misdeeds.

FLOOD

A well-known example is the story of Noah and the flood in Genesis 6–9. Waters that had provided the platform for the appearance of dry land are deliberately used to cover the dry ground. Water that misted the soil and flowed in channels or springs to nourish life escapes its boundaries and deluges all creation. As a natural disaster, a great flood would have been bad enough; worse, the cause of the flood is specifically divine punishment for human wickedness: "The LORD saw that the wickedness of humankind was great in the earth, and that every inclination of the thoughts of their hearts was only evil continually. And the LORD was sorry that he had made humankind on the earth, and it grieved him to his heart. So the LORD said, 'I will blot out from the earth the human beings I have created—people together with animals and creeping things and birds of the air, for I am sorry that I have made them'" (Gen 6:5–7). In God's first speech to Noah, God explains, "I have determined to make an end of all flesh, for the earth is filled with violence because of them; now I am going to destroy them along with the earth" (Gen 6:13). After Noah, his family, and representative animals are on the ark, and the water has risen, the narrator details the destruction: "And all flesh died that moved on the earth, birds, domestic animals, wild animals, all swarming creatures that swarm on the earth, and all human beings; everything on dry land in whose nostrils was the breath of life died. He blotted out every living thing that was on the face of the ground, human beings and animals and creeping things and birds of the air; they were blotted out from the earth" (Gen 7:21–23). Later, God makes a covenant with Noah never to destroy the earth again with a flood of water (on the theme of covenant, see chapter 2 below).

DROUGHT

In a desert culture, we should not be surprised that water is of great importance. In the cosmology of ancient Israel, the waters were gathered above the dome of the sky and below the land mass of the earth, poised above and below humanity to break forth in destruction. A more likely danger was the withholding of water from the sky, resulting in prolonged drought. Israel's neighbors in Egypt and Mesopotamia were nourished by the great river systems of the Nile or the Tigris and Euphrates. Irrigation canals leading from the rivers provided water for agricultural acreage to produce grain, fruits, and vegetables year-round. Not so in Israel. Israel's agriculture was entirely dependent on rainfall, so failed crops were only a dry spell away. The threat of drought, therefore, was deadly. One of the curses in Deuteronomy for failure to obey God's covenant is fiery heat and drought (Deut 28:22).

The punishment of drought plays an important role in the interaction of the prophet Elijah and King Ahab. When Elijah enters the biblical narrative, his first words are about drought: "Now Elijah the Tishbite, of Tishbe in Gilead, said to Ahab, 'As the LORD the God of Israel lives, before whom I stand, there shall be neither dew nor rain these years, except by my word'" (1 Kgs 17:1). Although the coming drought that Elijah predicts is not specifically designated as punishment against Ahab, the paragraph just before this verse, which introduces King Ahab, clearly characterizes him as someone who "did evil in the sight of the LORD more than all who were before him" (1 Kgs

16:30). Following his announcement, Elijah retreats to the wilderness, where he is fed by ravens and drinks from the wadi. "But after a while the wadi dried up, because there was no rain in the land" (1 Kgs 17:7). When Elijah travels to the northern seacoast of Sidon, he encounters a foreign widow scrounging for her last supper. When Elijah asks her for sustenance, she demurs with the pathos-filled response, "I have nothing baked, only a handful of meal in a jar, and a little oil in a jug; I am now gathering a couple of sticks, so that I may go home and prepare it for myself and my son, that we may eat it, and die" (1 Kgs 17:12). Clearly, the drought is punishing not just Ahab in the northern kingdom of Israel, but has reached deadly proportions in the southern desert and at the northern coast. At the beginning of the next chapter we learn that the drought lasted three years before God announced rainy relief.

Another prophet, Jeremiah, describes the devastating effects of drought on all creation:

> The word of the LORD that came to Jeremiah concerning the drought: Judah mourns and her gates languish; they lie in gloom on the ground, and the cry of Jerusalem goes up. Her nobles send their servants for water; they come to the cisterns, they find no water, they return with their vessels empty. They are ashamed and dismayed and cover their heads, because the ground is cracked. Because there has been no rain on the land the farmers are dismayed; they cover their heads. Even the doe in the field forsakes her newborn fawn because there is no grass. The wild asses stand on the bare heights, they pant for air like jackals; their eyes fail because there is no herbage. (Jer 14:1–6)

The following verse makes clear that the drought is punishment for human transgression of the covenant: "Although our iniquities testify against us, act, O LORD, for your name's sake; our apostasies indeed are many, and we have sinned against you" (Jer 14:7).

Likewise, the prophet Haggai, writing in the late sixth century BCE, chastises the people for neglecting the reconstruction of the Temple after their return from exile in Babylon. Apparently, they had been much more concerned with building their own houses than with building the house of God. The punishment for such neglect is drought: "And I have called for a drought on the land and the hills, on the grain, the new wine, the oil, on what the soil produces, on human beings and animals, and on all their labors" (Hag 1:11). If the people don't have crops and herds to care for, perhaps they will have time and energy to build God's temple.

PLAGUES

Another well-known use of creation as punishment for human wickedness is the Exodus plague narrative. Recounted in Exodus 7–12, the plagues punish the pharaoh (and the Egyptians) for refusing to let the Israelites leave the land as God has commanded. The plagues are signs that point to the surpassing supremacy of the God of Israel, and are inflicted so that "the Egyptians shall know that I am the LORD" (Exod 7:5). Just as some have accounted for the wilderness traditions of water from a rock, manna, and quail by pointing to natural processes, so some have explained the plagues by reference to natural phenomena (red algae in the Nile causes the frogs to leap out and die, which attracts gnats and flies, and so on).

Just as these speculations are a distraction when discussing the wilderness traditions, so such "natural" explanations for the plague narratives are beside the theological point. The story wants readers to attribute the plague to the God of Israel, who chooses to punish Pharaoh for his hardened heart. Elements of creation are called to play a destructive role in this drama. Life-giving water in the Nile is turned into undrinkable blood; frogs cover the land of Egypt and then die in heaps; gnats and flies and locusts come in swarms; boils break out on livestock and humans; hail rains down; darkness abandons its appointed time at night and overshadows the daylight. Creation has lost its structure and content so carefully ordered in the beginning, and the earth is on its way to becoming once again a formless void. Finally, water turns against the Pharaoh when the Egyptian army drowns in the Red Sea (Exod 14:28; 15:4–5).

FIRE AND OTHER DEVASTATIONS

Of particular note is the use of creative elements as agents of punishment in the prophets. Prophetic works are notoriously difficult to interpret since they are generally not narratives with a plot that can be easily followed from beginning to end. Rather, prophetic texts are typically poetic, oral announcements steeped in metaphor and simile, which by nature are open to various interpretations. Our interest here is in the prophetic use of creation language (whether metaphorical or literal) to threaten judgment or announce punishment. whether intended to be metaphorical or literal is of no consequence.

We begin with Amos, an eighth-century-BCE prophet denouncing the northern kingdom of Israel for rampant economic injustice and for practicing religious rituals without moral righteousness. The book of Amos opens with indictments of seven nations around Israel, each of which is accused of specific acts of wickedness. Yet the punishment for each is the same: God will send fire to punish that nation (Amos 1:4, 7, 10, 12, 14; 2:2, 5). Amos's indictment of Israel and its deserved punishment occupy the rest of the book. In chapter 4, five stanzas illustrate the lengths to which God has gone to avoid having to punish Israel. Each stanza poignantly ends with the refrain, "yet you did not return to me, says the Lord." The middle three stanzas specifically mention the divine use of created elements to bring Israel to her senses: "And I also withheld the rain from you when there were still three months to the harvest; I would send rain on one city, and send no rain on another city; one field would be rained upon, and the field on which it did not rain withered" (4:7); "I struck you with blight and mildew; I laid waste your gardens and your vineyards; the locust devoured your fig trees and your olive trees" (4:9); "I sent among you a pestilence after the manner of Egypt" (4:10). Locusts and fire reappear in the prophet's visions in chapter 7. There Amos sees locusts eating all the vegetation of the land (7:2) and a shower of fire devouring the deep and eating the land (7:4). Interpreting these visions of creation run amok as signs of God's judgment, Amos pleads for mercy on behalf of the people of Israel. In another episode, Amos sees a basket of summer fruit (Hebrew: *qayits*, pronounced "kites"), which is interpreted as a sign of the end (Hebrew: *qeyts*, pronounced "kates") of the people (8:2). (This Hebrew word-play uses the same consonants with different vowels; an English equivalent word-play would be interpreting a *broom* as a

sign that the divine cup of wrath was filled to the *brim*.)
The ultimate judgment on the people is their exile to a foreign land (7:17), a day so dreadful that "I will make the sun
go down at noon, and darken the earth in broad daylight"
(8:9). Divine use of the celestial bodies is possible because
the Lord is "the one who made the Pleiades and Orion,
and turns deep darkness into the morning, and darkens
the day into night" (5:8).

Hosea's prophecy was also directed toward the northern kingdom in the eighth century BCE. Hosea is perhaps
best known for his embodied metaphor of spiritual adultery, whereby he (representing God) relentlessly pursues
his promiscuous wife (representing Israel); description of
this pursuit in poignant prose fills the first three chapters
of the book of Hosea. The poetic chapters following these
indict Israel for chasing like a dove (7:11) or like a wild
donkey in heat (8:9) after other gods. Rather than being
a luxuriant vine (10:1) and the first fruits of the fig tree
(9:10), Israel has become poisonous weeds (10:4) and
a nonproductive stump (9:16). One passage in Hosea is
striking in its bluntness about the interconnectedness
between human behavior and the elements of creation:
"Hear the word of the LORD, O people of Israel; for the
LORD has an indictment against the inhabitants of the
land. There is no faithfulness or loyalty, and no knowledge
of God in the land. Swearing, lying, and murder, and stealing and adultery break out; bloodshed follows bloodshed.
Therefore the land mourns, and all who live in it languish;
together with the wild animals and the birds of the air,
even the fish of the sea are perishing" (4:1–3). The important prophetic phrase *'al-ken* ("therefore" or "on account of
this") regularly shows an explicit connection between the

accusation and the consequences. We are to understand, therefore, that because *humans* are breaking the commandments (swearing, deceiving, murdering, stealing, and committing adultery), the *land* and its *animal* inhabitants are suffering. In short, when we lie, fish die. For all who are concerned with the fragility of the web of life, this verse conveys a profound truth.

A few more examples will suffice to make the point. The work under the prophet Joel's name is placed canonically between Hosea and Amos; about Joel's historical chronology nothing is known for certain (scholars typically place him in the 400s BCE). Like Amos, he uses the metaphor of the locust as a sign of God's terrible judgment: "What the cutting locust left, the swarming locust has eaten. What the swarming locust left, the hopping locust has eaten, and what the hopping locust left, the destroying locust has eaten" (Joel 1:4; see also 2:25). The prophet Isaiah of Jerusalem (750–700 BCE) compares Judah to a beloved vineyard that has unexpectedly yielded wild grapes (5:1–2). As punishment, God says, "I will also command the clouds that they rain no rain upon it" (5:6b). Then a series of six woe oracles laments the behavior of the people, which will certainly lead to their death: "Therefore the anger of the LORD was kindled against his people, and he stretched out his hand against them and struck them; the mountains quaked, and their corpses were like refuse in the streets" (5:25). Even earthquakes may be summoned to punish God's people.

More examples from the Old Testament could be marshaled to illustrate the point that creation is used in punishing ways against humanity. More fruitful, perhaps, is brief consideration of the implications of this point.

How does the Old Testament understand the causal link between creation and moral behavior? While we do not have the space to take up that question in its entirety, we suggest in part that ancient Israel's confession of God as Creator of all allows some voices in the Bible to confess that the Creator can and does use creation for punishment of humanity. We do not suggest that this is a necessary next step for all who confess God as Creator; many of us would assert that elements of creation sometimes wreak havoc with no explicit divine intervention at all. In ancient Judah, Isaiah interpreted an earthquake as God's judgment on wicked human behavior. In contemporary California, an earthquake may be interpreted as the result of the shifting of tectonic plates along the San Andreas fault. At the very least, the Old Testament witnesses to the intricate interrelatedness of all creation. All humanity would do well to ponder the assertion, "When we lie, fish die."

CREATION IN THE END TIMES

Thus far we have considered the theme of creation in the Old Testament as it relates to the beginnings of the universe and its inhabitants, and as it relates to providence and punishment. In this section, we explore biblical eschatological visions, theological reflections, on the role of creation in restoration and in the end-times. Hebrew has no specific word like *eschaton* in Greek to denote the end-times. Instead, the stock phrase "on that day" is used to articulate ancient Israel's expectations of restoration and re-creation. The phrase is also used in a noneschatological sense to specify the particular day of an event; context determines the phrase's meaning.

Restoration

Judah's exile to Babylon in 587 BCE rent asunder the sociopolitical and religious institutions that grounded ancient Israel and provided its identity. In the destruction and exile, Israel lost her king, her temple, and her land. Remarkably, biblical writers articulated a vision of restoration that encompassed restoration of the exiled community back in the land, rule by a Davidic king, and worship in a rebuilt temple. Specifically, we are interested in what role creation plays in this vision of a restored community, so we turn to two significant prophets of the exile: Ezekiel, and Second Isaiah.

In his vision of the valley of dry bones, Ezekiel depicts the exiles as dry, scattered bones (Ezek 37:1–2, 11). The prophet sees the bones enlivened by the breath of God, joined with sinews, filled out with flesh, and covered with skin (Ezek 37:5, 8) and addressed by God's climactic promise: "I will put my spirit [breath] within you, and you shall live, and I will place you on your own soil" (Ezek 37:14a). God is depicted as a heart surgeon for Israel, who will "remove from your body the heart of stone and give you a heart of flesh" (Ezek 36:26). Further, God promises to "summon the grain and make it abundant" and "make the fruit of the tree and the produce of the field abundant" (Ezek 36:29, 30).

The prophet called Second Isaiah, believed to be primarily responsible for chapters 40–55 of the book of Isaiah, envisions a new exodus from Babylon, which will surpass the previous exodus from Egypt. The path from Babylon to Jerusalem will be passable because "every valley shall be lifted up, and every mountain and hill be made low; the uneven ground shall become level, and the rough places a plain" (Isa 40:4). Further, "I will open rivers on the bare heights, and fountains in the midst of the valleys; I will make the wilderness [*midbar*] a pool of water, and the dry land springs of water. I will put in the wilderness [*midbar*] the cedar, the acacia, the myrtle, and the olive; I will set in the desert the cypress, the plane and the pine together" (Isa 41:18–19; see also Isa 43:19–20; 44:3; 35:6b–7). The reverse will happen for those who trust in idols: "I will lay waste mountains and hills, and dry up all their herbage; I will turn the rivers into islands, and dry up the pools" (Isa 42:15; see also 50:2). Restoration to Zion or Jerusalem is compared to returning to the primeval garden: "For the LORD will comfort Zion; he will comfort all her waste places, and will make her wilderness [*midbar*] like Eden, her desert like the garden of the LORD" (Isa 51:3).

The vision of restoration "on that day" includes peace among former rivals in the animal kingdom: The wolf shall live with the lamb, the leopard shall lie down with the kid, the calf and the lion and a fatling together, and a little child shall lead them. The cow and the bear shall graze, their young shall lie down together; and the lion shall eat straw like the ox. The nursing child shall play over the hole of the asp, and the weaned child shall put its hand on the adder's den" (Isa 11:6–8). A similar peaceable kingdom is articulated by the prophet Ezekiel: "They [Israel] shall no more be plunder for the nations, nor shall the animals of the land devour them; but they shall live in safety, and no one shall make them afraid. I will provide for them a splendid vegetation so that they shall no more be consumed with hunger in the land" (Ezek 34:28–29; see also 36:29b–30). Peace will bring about sufficiency: "every one of you will eat from your own vine and your own fig tree, and drink water from your own cistern" (2 Kg 18:31; see also Joel 2:22; Zech 3:10).

Apocalyptic Re-Creation

The rehearsal of scholarship on the development of apocalyptic thought is too great an enterprise to undertake in this space. Suffice it for now to define apocalyptic notions of re-creation in the Old Testament as those texts that long for the time in the indeterminate future when cataclysmic divine intervention will restore the universe and its inhabitants to "the way things ought to be." The line between hopeful vision and apocalyptic eschatology is in many ways in the eye of the beholder. For our purposes, we point to two blocks of texts in the book of Isaiah and one block of texts in Ezekiel that seem to lean more toward apocalyptic eschatology than the ones discussed so far.

Ezekiel recounts his vision of the restored Jerusalem temple in chapters 40–48. After forty-six chapters devoted to surveying the dimensions and architecture of the temple in mind-numbing detail, Ezekiel is brought to the entrance to the temple where he sees water flowing from the temple in four directions. Astute readers will immediately recognize the allusion to Gen 2:10–14. The distinctiveness of Ezekiel's vision is that these waters are life restoring. The angelic messenger tells the prophet that the waters going toward the east will eventually flow into the Dead Sea, giving it life (Ezek 47:8). On both banks of the river will be trees for food, "whose leaves do not wither and whose fruit does not fail; for months they will bear first fruits because their waters go forth from the sanctuary. Their fruit will be for food and their leaves for healing" (Ezek 47:12). This is the final prophetic utterance by the prophet Ezekiel, a powerful vision of re-creation.

Isaiah 24–27 has been called "the Isaiah apocalypse" because the chapters portray an interest in classic apocalyptic themes: the eschatological banquet, universal judgment, heavenly portents, and the like. Naturally, elements of creation are involved, first in the devastation and then in the re-creation. The earth dries up and withers (Isa 24:4); the vine dries up and languishes (Isa 24:7); the foundations of the earth tremble so that the earth is utterly broken, torn asunder, and violently shaken (Isa 24:18b–19); the moon is abashed and the sun is ashamed (Isa 24:23a). At a divinely hosted banquet, the Lord will serve a feast of rich foods and fine wine (Isa 25:6). The transformation of the earth will be such that the Lord will "swallow up death forever" and "wipe away the tears from all faces" (Isa 25:4–5). Even more dramatic, the apocalyptic re-creation will allow the dead to live again: "Your dead shall live, their corpses shall rise. O dwellers in the dust, awake sing for joy" (Isa 26:19a).

The penultimate chapter of Isaiah also belongs to the literary category of proto-apocalyptic. On the trajectory that would eventuate in the vision of re-creation in Revelation 21, the prophet articulates a vision of a completely new creation.

> For I am about to create new heavens and a new earth; the former things shall not be remembered or come to mind. But be glad and rejoice forever in what I am creating; for I am about to create Jerusalem as a joy, and its people as a delight. I will rejoice in Jerusalem, and delight in my peo-

ple; no more shall a sound of weeping be heard
in it, or the cry of distress. No more shall there
be an infant that lives but a few days, or an old
person who does not live out a lifetime; for one
who dies at a hundred years will be considered a
youth, and one who falls short of a hundred will
be considered accursed. They shall build houses
and inhabit them; they shall plant vineyards and
eat their fruit . . . The wolf and the lamb shall feed
together, the lion shall eat straw like the ox; but
the serpent—its food shall be dust! They shall not
hurt or destroy on all my holy mountain, says the
LORD. (Isa 65:17–21, 25)

On that day, creation will be restored so that once again
God can say, "It is good."

Creation and Praise

We end with the recurring biblical theme that all creation gives praise to the Creator. Although not technically a function of the end-times, the image of creation's
praising God calls to mind a state of bliss that will only
be realized in the end-times. Lots of Hebrew words are
used to describe what the elements of creation will do.
Human praise of the Creator is manifested by obedience to the covenant (see chapter 2 below), worship (see
chapter 3 below), and ethical living (see chapter 4 below).
Wild animals, including cattle, creeping things, and flying
birds will praise [Hebrew: *hallel*] the LORD (Ps 148:10).
The English exclamation *hallelujah* (or *alleluia*) is the result of combining two Hebrew words: *Hallelu*, the plural
command "Praise," and *Yah*, the shortened form of God's
personal name YHWH. Wild beasts, jackals and ostriches

will honor God (Isa 43:20). Everything that breathes will praise the LORD and all flesh will worship God (Ps 150:6; Isa 66:23). All inhabitants of the earth and heavens will shout for joy (Jer 51:48). So far, so good. Anyone who has heard a child squeal with delight or a cat purr with contentment can easily resonate with living creatures offering verbal praise to God. More engaging is the biblical imagination that all elements of creation, not just sentient ones, praise the Creator.

The morning stars sing together while heavenly beings shout for joy (Job 38:7). The sun, moon, and stars praise and the heavens are glad and praise God's wonders and faithfulness (Ps 148:3; 96:11; 89:5). The heavens sing for joy (Isa 44:23). Likewise, the earth rejoices and exults, quakes, shouts for joy, and is full of praise (Ps 96:11; Isa 49:13; Ps 99:1; Isa 44:23; Hab 3:3). The land [*'adamah*] is glad and rejoices (Joel 2:21). The hills are girded with joy, sing for joy, praise, and sing (Ps 65:12; 98:8; 148:9; Isa 44:23; 49:13). The meadows and valleys shout for joy (Ps 65:13). Even the wilderness [*midbar*] praises God when it is glad, rejoices, sings for joy, and lifts up its voice (Isa 35:1-2; 42:11). Floods lift up their voice, roar, and clap their hands (Ps 93:3; 98:7–8; Isa 42:10). Likewise, the trees sing for joy, sing, and clap their hands (Ps 96:12; Isa 44:23; 55:12). Fire, hail, snow, frost, and wind praise the LORD (Ps 148:8). All of God's works bless the LORD, give thanks, and tell of the divine power and glory (Ps 103:22; 145:10–11). Would that all of us could hear the floods and trees clapping their hands and the wilderness singing for joy!

TWO

Covenant

A MAJOR THEME IN the Old Testament—some would say *the* major theme—is covenant as the metaphor used to describe the binding relationship between God and God's people. Whereas Hebrew uses a wide variety of words to talk about the theme of creation, only two Hebrew words carry the burden of talk about covenant. Used almost three hundred times, the word *berit* carries the connotation of treaty or contract, whereas the word *'edut*, used just over forty times, connotes testimony or witness. The Vulgate, the Latin Bible translation by Jerome in the fourth century CE, used the word *testamentum* most often to translate *berit* and *'edut*; this decision is reflected in the English title of the two parts of Christian Scripture as the Old and New Testaments. In this chapter, we will explore the ancient Near Eastern cultural context of covenants in order to be able to discern Israel's commonalities and discontinuities with the surrounding cultures. Then we will review some of the covenants enacted between humans in the Old Testament before turning to the major covenants established between God and humans.

ANCIENT NEAR EASTERN COVENANTS

Excavations from the ancient Near East have yielded a treasure trove of documents that provide a glimpse into the ancient world. As noted in the first chapter, creation stories from Mesopotamia shed light on the creation narratives of ancient Israel. Similarly, political treaties between nations shed light on Israel's understanding of the enduring relationship with the God of Israel. The simplest kind of ancient treaty is the "grant covenant," so called because one party simply grants benefits to another, usually as a reward for demonstrated loyalty or service. Typically, the benefit is land, since land was the tangible means of wealth in the ancient world. The grant covenant solemnizes the benevolence of one party toward another, with no stated responsibilities for the recipient of the grant. The implicit expected response of the recipient is continued loyalty, gratitude, and goodwill in the future. In ancient societies in which reciprocity formed the basis for virtually every relationship, banking goodwill for the future was a critical strategy for success.

The more complicated ancient political treaty was the suzerainty treaty, so called because it was enacted between unequal parties, with the less-powerful party, the vassal, submitting to the more-powerful party, the suzerain. Two clusters of documents are particularly instructive. The first are treaties involving the Hittites, a group from Asia Minor (modern Turkey) that engaged with peoples in the lands of the eastern Mediterranean (Syria, Canaan, etc.) from approximately 1500 to 1200 BCE. These Hittite suzerainty treaties follow a common pattern featuring six elements:

1. Preamble: the suzerain identifies himself, usually as the ruler of a territory, selected as such by a particular deity.

2. Historical Prologue: the suzerain describes events in the past that have led to the point of making the treaty today. These may include beneficial acts already undertaken on behalf of the vassal, or the suzerain may describe his beneficence to other vassals.

3. Stipulations: the suzerain specifies particular behaviors expressly commanded or prohibited for the vassal.

4. Provision for deposit: the suzerain calls for the deposit of the treaty in a secure location, often a temple, and may announce regulations about its regular public reading.

5. Witnesses: those who serve as solemn witnesses to the treaty oath are listed, including deities of both the suzerain and the vassal.

6. Blessings and curses: the consequences of keeping or breaking the treaty are enumerated in concrete terms.

The Old Testament does not contain treaties between God and Israel that conform exactly to the Hittite suzerainty treaties, but individual elements of these treaties are present throughout the Old Testament. For example, the Ten Commandments can be interpreted as fulfilling the first three elements: "I am the LORD your God [preamble], who brought you out of the land of Egypt, out of the house of slavery [historical prologue]. You shall have no other gods before me [stipulation]," and so forth (Exod 20:2–3). Placing the stone tablets in the ark may reflect the fourth element (provision for deposit). The blessings of long life and prosperity are frequently cited as benefits of keeping God's covenant (see, for example, Exod 19:5; Deut 6:3).

The second cluster of ancient documents, known as the vassal treaties of Esarhaddon, is instructive in the structure of the book of Deuteronomy. A bit of history will set the stage. Assyria arose as a powerful empire in the mid-eighth century BCE and controlled much of the ancient Near East until the early seventh century. The northern kingdom of Israel fell to Assyrian might in 721 BCE, and the southern kingdom of Judah became as a political vassal. King Esarhaddon (reigned 681–669 BCE) was the youngest son of Sennacherib, the king of Assyria who besieged Jerusalem (see 2 Kings 18–19). Structured in a pattern similar to the Hittite suzerainty treaties, the vassal treaties of Esarhaddon impose an oath of loyalty on his subjects, especially concerning his chosen successor. The book of Deuteronomy seems to follow this overall pattern of a loyalty oath to the God of Israel, using similar language to describe loyalty ("love") and treason ("hate"). If the first eleven chapters of Deuteronomy are understood as a preamble and historical prologue similar to those of a suzerainty treaty, then the stipulations are contained in chapters 12–26. Provisions for depositing and reading the covenant are scattered throughout Deuteronomy, as are references to the people as witnesses. Strikingly, Deuteronomy 28 opens with blessings for keeping the covenant (14 verses); these are followed by curses for breaking the covenant (54 verses). The final editing of the book of Deuteronomy as Moses's farewell address on the

plains of Moab, with the people poised to enter the promised land, positions the book as a sermonic exhortation
and mutes its treaty aspects. Nevertheless, political treaties
from the ancient Near East offer a cultural backdrop for
Israel's own understanding of its binding relationship with
the God of Israel.

COVENANTS BETWEEN HUMANS

As we have seen, political treaties were the common expression of binding relationship between leaders of nations in the ancient world. In this section, we examine Old
Testament examples of treaties enacted between leaders,
between leaders and their people, and between ordinary
people.

Leader-Leader Covenants

The first example demonstrates a covenant enacted between political leaders, similar to the Hittite suzerainty
treaty or the vassal treaty of Esarhaddon. When Solomon
becomes king of Israel and Judah, King Hiram of Tyre
sends his royal congratulations. The two monarchs negotiate a mutually beneficial economic agreement whereby
King Hiram will cut and deliver cedar and cypress timber
in exchange for wheat and oil: "There was peace between
Hiram and Solomon; and the two of them made a treaty
[*berit*]" (1 Kgs 5:12).

The second example depicts a political covenant
between King David and Abner, the power behind the
throne of Israel. The opening chapters of 2 Samuel nar-
rate the tensions involved in David's eventual kingship
over Israel and Judah. After the death of Saul (1 Samuel

31), "the people of Judah came, and there [at Hebron] they anointed David king over Judah" (2 Sam 2:4). Meanwhile, Abner, the commander of Saul's army, had taken Saul's son Ishbaal and "made him king over all Israel" (2 Sam 2:9). The next chapter's opening verse sets the scene for what is to unfold: "There was a long war between the house of Saul and the house of David; David grew stronger and stronger, while the house of Saul became weaker and weaker" (2 Sam 3:1). Seeing the advantage of being allied with David, "Abner sent messengers to David at Hebron, saying, 'To whom does the land belong? Make your covenant [berit] with me, and I will give you my support to bring all Israel over to you'" (2 Sam 3:12). David makes a covenant with Abner and stipulates that his own wife Michal, Saul's daughter, be returned to him (2 Sam 3:13). As king maker, Abner is the de facto leader of Israel and able to negotiate covenants on its behalf.

In the next example, the initiation of the covenant comes from the vassal. After being attacked by the king of Israel, King Asa of Judah petitions the suzerain, King Ben-hadad of Syria, to come to his aid. The delegation from King Asa brings "all the silver and gold that were left in the treasures of the house of the LORD and the treasures of the king's house," and makes a request of King Ben-hadad: "Let there be an alliance [berit] between me and you, like that between my father and your father: I am sending you a present of silver and gold; go, break your alliance [berit] with King Baasha of Israel, so that he may withdraw from me" (1 Kgs 15:18–19). Apparently, Asa's petition was successful, for Syria's army came to Judah's aid.

The next time we encounter King Ben-hadad, he is leading his Syrian army, along with the armies of thirty-two other kings, against the army of Israel. When the Syrian army is defeated in two separate skirmishes, the tables are turned, and King Ben-hadad, the former suzerain, petitions the king of Israel, the former vassal, for leniency. The king of Israel agrees to the terms, "So he made a treaty [*berit*] with him and let him go" (1 Kgs 20:34).

Leader-People Covenants

A variation on the political suzerainty treaty between leaders is the treaty between a leader, on the one hand, and individuals not explicitly named as political leaders, on the other hand. For example, King Abimelech of the southern coastal area enters into a covenant first with Abraham (Gen 21:25–34) and then with Abraham's son Isaac (Gen 26:26–33) to resolve disputes over the access rights to wells. The narrative is likely a doublet (a single tradition told as two distinct stories) since each text ends with a linguistic explanation of the place name *Beer-Sheba*. In the Abrahamic version, Abraham gives seven ewe lambs to Abimelech so that he can be a witness to the covenant. (The need for covenant witnesses we saw as an element in the suzerainty treaties.) In the Isaac narrative, the men seal the covenant with a meal together, an element we will see repeated in the divine-human covenants (see below). Perhaps readers are to understand from each of these narratives that Abraham and Isaac are the leaders of their people and, therefore, enacting covenants on their behalf.

The Old Testament has many examples of leaders explicitly enacting covenants with people as groups. Once Joshua had established himself as the military leader of Israel with victories at Jericho and Ai, the inhabitants of

Gibeon (less than ten miles southeast of Ai) "went to Joshua in the camp at Gilgal [very near Jericho], and said to him and to the Israelites, 'We have come from a far country; so now make a treaty [*berit*] with us'" (Josh 9:6). Even though Joshua suspects the petitioners may be from a nearer area, "Joshua made peace with them, guaranteeing their lives by a treaty [*berit*]; and the leaders of the congregation swore an oath to them" (Josh 9:15). When Joshua's suspicions of deception are confirmed, he upholds the covenant by letting the Gibeonites live, but he punishes them by making them "hewers of wood and drawers of water" (Josh 9:21).

In a familiar scene from the last chapter of the book of Joshua, the people of Israel are gathered in Shechem in the central hill country. Joshua recounts what might be called their salvation history, and he exhorts the people: "Now if you are unwilling to serve the LORD, choose this day whom you will serve, whether the gods your ancestors served in the region beyond the River [Euphrates] or the gods of the Amorites [Canaanites] in whose land you are living; but as for me and my household, we will serve the LORD" (Josh 24:15). The people declare their choice to serve the LORD, and Joshua confirms: "You are witnesses against yourselves that you have chosen the LORD, to serve him" (Josh 24:22). "So Joshua made a covenant [*berit*] with the people that day, and made statutes and ordinances for them at Shechem. Joshua wrote these words in the book of the law of God; and he took a large stone, and set it up there under the oak in the sanctuary of the LORD" (Josh 24:25–26) as a witness to the covenant. In this passage, we see many elements of the suzerainty treaty: preamble, historical prologue, stipulations, public deposit, and witnesses. Many scholars believe this text reflects an actual covenant ceremony enacted each year at the sacred town of Shechem.

In a narrative of political intrigue surrounding the successor to King Ahaziah of Judah, his mother Athaliah determines to seize power by disposing of any royal pretenders to the throne. Her plot is foiled when the dead king's sister manages to hide one of the king's son, Joash/Jehoash, in the temple, where he alone escapes the mass murder. In the seventh year of his secret captivity in the temple, the priest Jehoiada "summoned the captains of the Carites [mercenaries] and of the guards and had them come to him in the house of the LORD. He made a covenant [*berit*] with them and put them under oath in the house of the LORD; then he showed them the king's son" (2 Kgs 11:4). With all these men armed and standing guard around Joash/Jehoash, the priest Jehoiada "brought out the king's son, put the crown on him, and gave him the covenant [*'edut*]; they proclaimed him king, and anointed him; they clapped their hands and shouted, 'Long live the king!'" (2 Kgs 11:12). The use of the two different Hebrew words for "covenant" is instructive here. The *berit* is the treaty enacted between the priest and the guards; the *'edut* is the evidence of the *berit*, although what was actually given to the new king is unclear.

In the last days of the kingdom of Judah, when King Nebuchadnezzar of Babylon had already begun to besiege Jerusalem, King Zedekiah of Judah "made a covenant [*berit*] with all the people in Jerusalem to make a proclamation of liberty to them, that all should set free their Hebrew slaves, male and female, so that no one should hold another Judean in slavery" (Jer 34:8–9). After initially agreeing, the people renege on their covenant and take slaves again, for which Jeremiah delivers a strong announcement of judgment (Jer 34:11–22).

People-People Covenants

If leaders can enter into covenants with other leaders and with people, then we will not be surprised to see that covenants are also made between people as individuals and people as groups. Many will recall the abiding friendship between David and Saul's son Jonathan, described on three occasions as "covenant" [*berit*]. The first occasion is set immediately after David's improbable defeat of Goliath: "When David had finished speaking to Saul, the soul of Jonathan was bound to the soul of David, and Jonathan loved him as his own soul . . . Then Jonathan made a covenant with David, because he loved him as his own soul" (1 Sam 18:1, 3). Later David begins to fear Saul's intentions toward him, flees from the palace, and implores Jonathan to cover for him that night at dinner. He appeals to their covenantal bond: "Therefore deal kindly with your servant, for you have brought your servant into a sacred covenant with you" (1 Sam 20:8a). When it becomes apparent to Jonathan that his father will soon be deposed as king, he finds David in the wilderness at Horesh and acknowledges David's imminent kingship: "Then the two of them made a covenant before the LORD; David remained at Horesh and Jonathan went home" (1 Sam 23:18). We learn from this extended narrative that the *berit* can be more than a political expediency; the motive can be love. Such a bond is described as "sacred" (the Hebrew says literally, "*berit* of YHWH") and is renewed "before the LORD."

The extended narrative about the tensions between Jacob and his uncle Laban ends with the two men making a covenant: "Come now, let us make a covenant [*berit*], you and I; and let it be a witness [*'ed*] between you and me" (Gen 31:44). The Hebrew word *'ed* (translated as "witness") is related to one of the words for "covenant": *'edut*. Then, Jacob sets up a pillar, and Laban and he gather stones into a heap, whereupon Laban proclaims, "This heap is a witness [*'ed*] between you and me today" (Gen 31:48). Laban further says, "See this heap and see the pillar, which I have set between you and me. This heap is a witness [*'ed*] and the pillar is a witness [*'edah*]" (Gen 31:51–52). The two men conclude their covenant ceremony with a sacrifice and a meal together (Gen 31:54), common actions to seal a covenant.

When modern readers consider the biblical notion of covenant, many recognize marriage as the most similar enactment of the ancient covenant in today's society. The prophet Malachi accuses the people of breaking the covenant of marriage, thus prompting God to reject their offerings at the temple: "You ask, 'Why does he not [accept our offerings]?' Because the LORD was a witness [*'ed*] between you and the wife of your youth, to whom you have been faithless, though she is your companion and your wife by covenant [*berit*]" (Mal 2:14).

Finally, we consider the possibility of groups of people making covenants with each other. Moses tells the people of Israel to "make no covenant [*berit*] with them," the inhabitants of the promised land, apparently prohibiting marrying their daughters and sons or worshiping their gods (Deut 7:1–5). Joshua will later remind the people of this divine instruction: "For your part, do not make a covenant [*berit*] with the inhabitants of this land; tear down their altars" (Judg 2:2).

COVENANTS BETWEEN GOD AND HUMANS

We are ready to turn now to texts in the Old Testament about the divine covenants. Texts will be discussed in canonical order; questions of authorship and chronology of composition will be put aside. That is, our aim is not to make a diachronic presentation of the development of covenants but instead to investigate what biblical texts in their final canonical form say about God's making covenants with humans.

God's Covenant with Noah

The first use of the word "covenant" [*berit*] in the Old Testament occurs in God's announcement to Noah about the coming flood. Noting that the wickedness of the earth had become excessive, God determines to blot out all living things, with the exception of Noah, his family, and some representative animals. "But I will establish my covenant with you; and you shall come into the ark, you, your sons, your wife, and your sons' wives with you" (Gen 6:18). The narrator says, "And God made a wind blow over the earth" (Gen 8:1), recalling the wind from God that swept over the face of the waters at the beginning. After the waters have receded enough for Noah to exit the ark, he builds an altar and offers whole burnt offerings to the LORD (Gen 8:20). The pleasing odor causes the LORD to relent from causing future destruction (Gen 8:21). The important ninth chapter of Genesis begins with God's blessing of Noah and his sons: "Be fruitful and multiply, and fill the earth. The fear and dread of you shall rest on every animal of the earth, and on every bird of the air, on everything that creeps on the ground, and on all the fish of the sea; into your hand they are delivered. Every moving thing that lives shall be food for you; and just as I gave you the green plants, I give you everything. Only, you shall not eat flesh with its life, that is, its blood" (Gen 9:1–4). Careful readers will note language very similar to the language in the first chapter of Genesis (especially from Gen 1:28–30). God establishes the covenant with Noah in Gen 9:8–17, quoted in its entirety here, with significant words italicized, boldfaced, underlined, or double underlined:

> Then God said to Noah and to his sons with him, "As for me, I am establishing <u>my</u> **covenant** with you and your descendants after you, and with every living creature that is with you, the birds, the domestic animals, and every animal of the earth with you, as many as came out of the ark. I establish <u>my</u> **covenant** with you, that never again shall all flesh be cut off by the waters of a flood, and never again shall there be a flood to destroy the earth." God said, "This is the *sign of the* **covenant** that I make between me and you and every living creature that is with you, for all future generations: I have set my bow in the clouds, and it shall be a *sign of the* **covenant** between me and the earth. When I bring clouds over the earth and the bow is seen in the clouds, I will remember <u>my</u> **covenant** that is between me and you and every living creature of all flesh; and the waters shall never again become a flood to destroy all flesh. When the bow is in the clouds, I will see it and remember the <u>everlasting</u> **covenant** between God and every living creature of all flesh that is

> on the earth." God said to Noah, "This is the *sign of the* **covenant** that I have established between me and all flesh that is on the earth."

In the space of ten verses, the word *covenant* appears seven times. Three times it is preceded by "my," three times by "sign of the," and once by "everlasting." The careful use of these words seven and three times shows an interest in signaling the perfect completeness of God's covenant with Noah. The universality of the covenant is emphasized by the use of the Hebrew word *kol* ("all" or "every") twelve times in the ten verses. (The English translation above uses "all" or "every" only ten times, ignoring two uses of the Hebrew word near the end of v. 10.) This precise structuring of the passage points to its deliberate literary composition; its literariness makes it similar to the deliberate liturgy of Genesis 1. Recall the seven days of creation, seven pronouncements of "good," three uses of "separate," and three blessings in Genesis 1. Scholars therefore attribute the overall structure of the flood narrative in Genesis to the Priestly source—to the same source as Genesis 1. Apparently, the conflicting information about the numbers of animals taken on board the ark (seven pairs or one pair) and the length of the flood (forty days or seven months) results from less-than-stellar editing of the available sources.

The covenant with Noah does not exhibit explicit similarities with the suzerain treaties discussed above, although some elements of similarity may be noted. The preamble and historical prologue are understood implicitly in the mention of the ark; that is, God is the one who has brought Noah and his family safely through the deluge by means of the ark. God makes no apparent stipulation for Noah to follow. God does not command or prohibit anything in this passage. But this text is clearly the conclusion to the larger narrative introduced by the pre-announcement of the covenant in Gen 6:18. In that sense, therefore, God's prohibition of eating blood in Gen 9:4 serves as the stipulation of the covenant. Blessing for fulfilling the covenant is understood in Gen 9:1; curses are imposed in God's "reckoning" of life for life in Gen 9:5–6. The "sign of the covenant" fulfills the provision for deposit and public reading, as well as the role of witness to the covenant. God says, "I have set my bow in the clouds" (Gen 9:13). This is the normal Hebrew word for "bow," as in "bow and arrow" (see, for example, Gen 21:20 where Ishmael is described as an expert with the bow). The word does not explicitly mean a rainbow; the fact that the bow is hung in the sky and appears after rain gives us the composite word "rainbow." In its cultural context, the text is saying that God has hung up the divine weapon of war (the bow) and will not again undertake to destroy creation. Logically, the connection between the bow (and arrow) and the flood is difficult to determine. Culturally, however, other ancient Near Eastern narratives shed light on this text.

Recall the Mesopotamian story *Enuma Elish*, in which Marduk kills Tiamat by shooting an arrow from his bow into her body (see chapter 1 above). After he uses her body parts to create the universe, Marduk hangs up his bow in the clouds as a sign of his commitment to abandoning war. Recall also the *Epic of Athrahasis*, in which humanity is formed from a mixture of clay, blood, and spittle to serve the gods (see chapter 1 above). After six hundred years, the human population had increased to dangerous levels, so the gods sent a flood to wipe out humanity. Enki, the god of the waters underneath the earth, warns Atrakhasis to build a large boat big enough to survive the impending deluge. The flood lasts seven days and nights, destroying everything except Atrakhasis, his family, and his livestock. After disembarking on dry land, Atrakhasis offers burnt offerings to the gods in thanksgiving, which attract the gods like flies.

The most notable parallel to the Genesis flood narrative is the *Epic of Gilgamesh*, a Babylonian literary masterpiece from ca. 2000 BCE. Gilgamesh, the king of Uruk, a prominent city on the Persian Gulf, is two-thirds divine and one-third human. He engages in several adventures with a primitive god-man named Enkidu, and the two become fast friends. When Enkidu dies, Gilgamesh becomes despondent over his own mortality, and undertakes a visit to Utnapishtim. Like Noah, Utnapishtim is a survivor of a great flood, and his tale has many similarities to Genesis, including the rescue of Utnaptishtim's family and animals, the use of birds to determine the recession of the waters, and whole burnt offerings as thanksgiving for survival. Unlike Noah, Utnapishtim is granted immortality as a reward. When Gilgamesh finally reaches him after many trials and tribulations, Utnapishtim tells him about a plant with rejuvenating powers. Gilgamesh secures the plant only to lose it on the way back to Uruk; its loss leaves him more despondent than when he started.

Surprisingly, the covenant with Noah is not commonly referenced in the rest of the Old Testament. Its use in Isaiah 54 instills confidence in God's compassion to the exiles: "This is like the days of Noah to me: Just as I swore that the waters of Noah would never again go over the earth, so I have sworn that I will not be angry with you and will not rebuke you" (Isa 54:9). Noah is mentioned, along with Daniel and Job, as models of righteousness in Ezekiel 14. Of course, flood is an apt metaphor in the psalms and prophets for overwhelming destruction, but there is no clear reference to *the* flood in any of those books.

God's Covenant with Abraham

Abraham (as Abram) steps onto the biblical stage in Genesis 12 as part of the *toledot* of Terah (see chapter 1 above) and will be the main protagonist for thirteen chapters. Recipient of God's promises and party to God's covenant, Abraham lives in the biblical imagination as the patriarch par excellence. Most readers familiar with the story of Abraham, when asked to point to God's covenant with him, would point to Gen 12:1–3: "Now the LORD said to Abram, 'Go from your country ['*erets*] and your kindred and your father's house to the land ['*erets*] that I will show you. I will make of you a great nation, and I will bless you, and make your name great, so that you will be a blessing. I will bless those who bless you, and the one who curses you I will curse; and in you all the families of the earth shall be blessed.'" In the strictest sense, God's blessing to Abram at this point does not include possession of the land. The strict literalist will note that Abram is to go to another land where God's blessing will be manifest in descendants, the ancient means to "a great nation" that makes its "name great." Four verses later, "Then the LORD appeared to Abram, and said, 'To your offspring I will give this land.' So he built there an altar to the LORD, who had appeared to him" (Gen 12:7). Note that there is no use of the word *covenant* here; rather, the operative verbs are *bless* and *give*. Abram accepts the promise of God as spoken until chapter 15, when Abram voices his impatience with God, flatly complaining, "You have given me no offspring" (Gen 15:3). The divine promise is repeated when "he [the LORD] brought him outside and said, 'Look toward heaven and count the stars, if you are able to count them.' Then he said to him, 'So shall your descendants be'" (Gen 15:5). The narrator confirms for readers, "And he believed the LORD; and the LORD reckoned it to him as righteousness" (Gen 15:6).

In the next verse readers encounter the divine promise: "I am the LORD who brought you from Ur of the Chaldeans, to give you this land to possess" (Gen 15:7). Once again, Abram questions the promise, at which time the LORD and Abram perform a ritual ceremony. Animals are cut in half and arranged with an aisle between the halves (Gen 15:9–10). "When the sun had gone down and it was dark, a smoking fire pot and a flaming torch passed between these pieces. On that day the LORD made [*karat*] a covenant [*berit*] with Abram, saying, 'To your descendants I give this land'" (Gen 15:17–18). Here is the actual enactment of the covenant with Abram. The verb used in this instance is the verb *karat*: "cut." One would expect the Hebrew verb "establish" or "set" or even "covenant." But approximately one-third of the uses of *berit* use "cut" to describe the enactment of the covenant. Scholars posit that this ritual cutting ceremony may lie behind the expression "cut a covenant." A similar ceremony is referenced in Jeremiah 34, where the prophet condemns the people for reneging on a covenant they had undertaken to free all Hebrew slaves.

And those who transgressed my covenant and
did not keep the terms of the covenant that they
made before me, I will make like the calf when
they cut it in two and passed between its parts:
the officials of Judah, the officials of Jerusalem, the
eunuchs, the priests, and all the people of the land
who passed between the parts of the calf shall be
handed over to their enemies and to those who
seek their lives. Their corpses shall become food
for the birds of the air and the wild animals of the
earth. (Jer 34:18–20)

Scholars believe that Genesis 15 preserves an ancient
covenant ceremony in which the one taking on the covenant responsibilities walked the aisle between the cut animals as if to say, "If I do not keep the covenant I am making
today, may I be like these animals: cut open and left for the
birds of prey." In this instance, the smoking firepot and the
flaming torch obviously represent God; Abram is a silent
partner in the covenant ceremony: the recipient of divine
blessing with no explicit reciprocal responsibilities.

Careful readers will have noted that the promise that
Abram will possess the land varies in these texts. In Gen
12:7, the gift of land is promised not to Abram per se, but
to his descendants. In Gen 15:7 the promise is specifically
to Abram, with inheritance by descendants presumed. In
Gen 15:18 (the explicit declaration of the covenant), the
gift is specifically to Abram's descendants. Even though the
explicit covenant gift is land, by virtue of God's including
as recipients Abram's descendants (of which he has none),
readers are to understand that the covenant also includes
the gift of offspring. The final form of Genesis was com-
piled from many traditions and edited over centuries so

that such literal distinctions are smoothed over in readers' minds. The covenant tradition memorialized in Genesis 15 is typically attributed to the J (or Yahwist) source since it uses the name LORD and preserves this ancient ritual. The story has a kind of "you are there" quality to it, with details about the kinds of animals needed and how to cut them. One can actually visualize Abram carefully laying out these animal carcasses and then acting as a human scarecrow to keep the birds of prey from disrupting his ritual arrangement. The covenant with Abram preserved in Genesis 15 has characteristics of the ancient "grant" covenant formalizing the gift of land from the more powerful party to a beneficiary. The formal structure of the suzerainty treaty is absent, although the suzerain does self-identify and provide an abbreviated historical prologue. There are no stipulations, there are no witnesses, and there is no lasting legacy for public reading. Since there are no explicit stipulations, there can be no articulated blessings and curses for failure to keep the stipulations. The only curse in the text is the implicit curse on the suzerain, symbolized by the cut animals.

A parallel tradition of the covenant with Abram appears in Genesis 17; it is composed of three parts: God's covenant with Abram (vv. 1–14), implications for Abram's wife and sons (vv. 15–22), and Abram's fulfillment of covenant stipulations (vv. 23–27). The first part is structured as a suzerainty treaty and betrays interests associated with the Priestly source, as well as similarities with both the creation liturgy of Genesis 1 and the covenant with Noah in Genesis 9. Again note emphasized words:

When Abram was ninety-nine years old, the
LORD appeared to Abram, and said to him, "I am
God Almighty; walk before me, and be blameless.
And I will make <u>my</u> **covenant** between me and
you, and will make you exceedingly numerous."
Then Abram fell on his face; and God said to him,
"As for me, this is <u>my</u> **covenant** with you: You
shall be the ancestor of a multitude of nations. No
longer shall your name be Abram, but your name
shall be Abraham; for I have made you the ancestor of a multitude of nations. I will make you
exceedingly fruitful; and I will make nations of
you, and kings shall come from you. I will establish <u>my</u> **covenant** between me and you, and your
offspring after you throughout their generations,
for an <u>everlasting</u> **covenant**, to be God to you and
to your offspring after you. And I will give to you,
and to your offspring after you, the land where
you are now an alien, all the land of Canaan, for
a perpetual holding; and I will be their God."
God said to Abraham, "As for you, you shall keep
<u>my</u> **covenant**, you and your offspring after you
throughout their generations. This is <u>my</u> **covenant**, which you shall keep, between me and you
and your offspring after you: Every male among
you shall be circumcised. You shall circumcise
the flesh of your foreskins, and it shall be a *sign of
the* **covenant** between me and you. Throughout
your generations every male among you shall be
circumcised when he is eight days old, including
the slave born in your house and the one bought
with your money from any foreigner who is not
of your offspring. Both the slave born in your
house and the one bought with your money must
be circumcised. So shall <u>my</u> **covenant** be in your
flesh an <u>everlasting</u> **covenant**. Any uncircum-

cised male who is not circumcised in the flesh of
his foreskin shall be cut off from his people; he
has broken <u>my</u> **covenant**." (Gen 17:1–14)

As we saw with Genesis 1 and 9, the author has carefully composed the text. The word "covenant" appears ten
times; tenfold repetition was a common mnemonic device
for memorization of the text. "Covenant" is preceded by
"my" seven times, by "everlasting" two times, and by "sign
of the" one time. Language of fruitfulness recalls the blessing in Gen 1:28. The repetition of "between me and you
and your offspring" recalls the covenant with Noah in Gen
9:8–17. The sign of the covenant here is circumcision of all
males, whether freeborn or slave, whether foreign or na-
tive. Later, the Passover instructions will cover these same
categories (Exod 12:43–49). The divine suzerain self-identifies as 'el shaddai. The first word is the common Semitic
word for deity, but the etymology and exact meaning of
the second word is uncertain. In cognate Semitic lan-
guages, the supposed roots mean "deal violently" or "pour
forth" or "high." By convention, most scholars translate the
phrase as "God Almighty." To recall the treaty elements,
no historical prologue recounts the benevolent actions for
Abram, who is enjoined to circumcise all males throughout the generations. Abraham's new name, linguistically
associated with "father of a multitude," will serve as public
reminder of God's covenant promise. Blessings for keeping the covenant include descendants and land; the curse
for not keeping it is to be cut off from the people. Readers
can appreciate the irony that not being cut in circumcision
results in being cut off.

By the end of chapter 15, divine promises initially characterized as "blessings" in chapter 12 are finalized and remembered as "covenant." Covenant promises include land and descendants. So readers are surprised by Abram's very next encounter with God and the recounting of this parallel covenant tradition in chapter 17. Only seventeen verses have passed since the strange story with cut animals and a smoking fire pot, and now God shows up to make another covenant with Abram? Granted, thirteen years have passed in Abram's life, but this is the first reported conversation with Abram that God has had since the promise to give his descendants the land. Why would God need to make another covenant with Abram to grant him descendants and land yet again? The answers are found in the intervening chapter, where Ishmael is born to Abram and Hagar, Sarai's Egyptian maid. After harsh treatment from Sarai, Hagar and Ishmael run away to the wilderness, where an angel of the LORD promises to protect them and commands them to return to Abram's camp. Although their return is not described, every reader knows that angels are to be obeyed. But this leaves the problem (from the Israelite perspective) of a Israelite-Egyptian son as the sole heir to land and descendants. This tension is resolved by the assurance of another son to Abram in chapter 17: a son through whom the covenant will be fulfilled. In verses 15–22, the word *covenant* appears three times; two uses of "my" covenant bookend one use of "everlasting" covenant. Both Abraham's sons will have the blessing of descendants, but only Isaac will bear the fullness of the covenant promise of land. The final section of the chapter assures readers that Abraham undertook the covenant stipulation, circumcising all the males of his household. Interestingly, we are told three times that Ishmael was circumcised (vv. 23, 25, 26), but we are left to ponder what this will mean as descendants multiply and interact.

In language reminiscent of God's promise to Abraham in Gen 12:1–3, the covenant is passed on to Isaac: "Reside in this land as an alien, and I will be with you, and will bless you; for to you and to your descendants I will give all these lands, and I will fulfill the oath that I swore to your father Abraham. I will make your offspring as numerous as the stars of heaven, and will give to your offspring all these lands; and all the nations of the earth shall gain blessing for themselves through your offspring" (Gen 26:3–4). Even though the word *berit* is not used in the remainder of Genesis to refer to the Abrahamic covenant, the phrase "the oath that I swore to your father" serves as a synonym for the covenant promise. The covenant is passed on to Isaac's son Jacob in a dream: "And the LORD stood beside him and said, 'I am the LORD, the God of Abraham your father and the God of Isaac; the land on which you lie I will give to you and to your offspring; and your offspring shall be like the dust of the earth, and you shall spread abroad to the west and to the east and to the north and to the south; and all the families of the earth shall be blessed in you and in your offspring'" (Gen 28:13–14). Even though the later story of Joseph takes up more than one-quarter of the book of Genesis (chapters 37–50), the covenant of his fathers is never passed on to him. The biblical tradition remembers the oath made to the ancestors Abraham, Isaac, and Jacob.

The divine covenant with the ancestors will be tested when the descendants of Jacob find themselves in Egypt. What had started as sojourning in "the best part" of an hospitable land (Gen 47:5–6) becomes harsh slavery, on account of which the Israelites groan and cry out in distress (Exod 2:23). Readers know that Israel's fortunes are about to take a turn for the better when "God heard their groaning, and God remembered his covenant [*berit*] with Abraham, Isaac, and Jacob" (Exod 2:24). That is, the role of Moses as liberating agent is set under the auspices of the Abrahamic covenant. God's promise to give the land of Canaan to Abraham's descendants is not yet fulfilled, so God announces to Moses, "I have come down to deliver them from the Egyptians, and to bring them up out of that land to a good and broad land, a land flowing with milk and honey, to the country of the Canaanites," and the other Semitic peoples of the land (Exod 3:8). In a parallel tradition in Exodus chapter 6, God remembers the covenant already established with Abraham and promises, "I will bring you into the land that I swore to give to Abraham, Isaac, and Jacob; I will give it to you for a possession. I am the LORD" (Exod 6:8). Readers interpret the burning bush episode in its current form as Moses's initial call, and the call in chapter 6 as recommissioning or reassurance after Moses' initial encounter with Pharaoh in chapter 5. Also, we note here the biblical stock phrase or 'code language' for the covenant: "I will take you as my people, and I will be your God" (Exod 6:7). The core of the covenantal promise is "I will be your God and you will be my people" (see, for example, Lev 26:12; Jer 7:23; 11:4; 30:22; Ezek 36:28). Literally, the Hebrew says, "I will become God for you and you will become people for me." The language of "become" indicates a process of growing in relationship not immediately obvious in the English. Also, the Hebrew indicates the benefit of the relationship: God for you and people for me. There is willingness in the relationship that may be obscured by the English pronouns *your* and *my*. The biblical notion of covenant is essentially relational and beneficial in nature.

God's Covenant at Sinai

The covenant at Sinai is arguably the most important in the Old Testament. Just over one-third of the Pentateuch is situated geographically at Mt Sinai. The rescued slaves arrive at Mount Sinai in Exod 19:1 and depart in Num 10:33, camped there at the mountain for twenty-one chapters in Exodus, twenty-seven chapters in Leviticus, and ten chapters in Numbers. With Genesis and Deuteronomy supplying prologue and epilogue to the story, the stay at Mount Sinai is the centerpiece of the Pentateuch. The complex editing of the Sinai events means that we cannot examine the uses of the words *berit* or *'edut* in the chronological order that the text presents. Rather, we will start with the Ten Commandments and work out from there, followed by a brief discussion of the ark of the covenant.

THE TEN COMMANDMENTS

To say "the Ten Commandments" is to epitomize the Sinai covenant. Conversations between Moses and Aaron and God are numerous in Exodus 3–19. But the oral proclamation of the commandments is the first time in the book of Exodus that the people have heard from God directly. And in fact, they are so terrified by the experience that they do not ever want it to happen again! The stone tablets, on which the commandments are chiseled, form bookends around the blasphemous incident of the golden calf. The Ten Commandments may function like chapter headings or file folders, since they are followed by numerous other commandments that further specify behavior. The Ten Commandments have been interpreted as "timeless truths"—commandments for all times and all peoples—whereas other laws are interpreted by some faith communities as time bound and culturally conditioned, applicable only to those people at that time. Paying close attention to the text, we note that the introduction at Exod 20:1 is, "Then God spoke all these words." They are not called commandments and are not listed as ten at this point. There is no mention of a covenant. There is no obvious marker that anything special is about to be said. Only when we get to chapter 24 of Exodus do we learn that God has used these words to make another covenant.

Scholars recognize Exodus 24 to be a mosaic (pun intended) of sources. The final editor has included at least three different traditions in such a way that readers are unsure what is happening where with whom. At times Moses comes down the mountain before he goes up, and vice versa. The first tradition is related in two parts, Exod 24:1–2 and vv. 9–11. God calls a delegation to come up the mountain: Moses, Aaron, Nadab, Abihu, and seventy elders (vv. 1–2). When the first story resumes in v. 9 after an interruption by the second tradition, readers are told, "and they saw the God of Israel. Under his feet there was something like a pavement of sapphire stone, like the very heaven for clearness. God did not lay his hand on the chief men of the people of Israel; also they beheld God, and they ate and drank" (Exod 24:10–11). Scholars believe this to be a very early tradition, because, remarkably, the men see God and live to tell about it. Later biblical tradition would come to understand that no one could ever see God and live (see Judg 13:22).

The second tradition in the chapter contains the word "covenant" [*berit*] twice. After Moses reports all the "words of the LORD" to the people, he sets up twelve pillars and slaughters animals to use for burnt offerings: "Then he took the book of the covenant, and read it in the hearing of the people; and they said, 'All that the LORD has spoken we will do, and we will be obedient.' Moses took the blood and dashed it on the people, and said, 'See the blood of the covenant that the LORD has made with you in accordance with all these words'" (Exod 24:7–8). In this context, readers naturally understand the book of the covenant to be all the words spoken by God from Exod 20:2 to Exod 23:33: that is, the Ten Commandments and all the laws that follow. The Hebrew word *sefer* ("book" or, more accurately, "document") implies a written text. But the stone tablets are not reported as given to Moses until the end of chapter 31, not to mention that two portable stone tablets could not possibly have room to record three chapters of laws. Most scholars therefore understand the phrase "book of the covenant" to be an anachronism, a retrojection of later legal codes into the episode at Mount Sinai. Moses then uses the blood from the sacrificial offerings to dash against the altar and over the assembly, purifying both (see chapter 3 below). Called specifically the "blood of the covenant," this ritual action apparently obligates the assembly to obedience above and beyond their verbal assent.

The third tradition, Exod 24:12–18, describes the LORD's summoning Moses up the mountain: "and I will give you the tablets of stone, with the law and the commandment, which I have written for their instruction"

(Exod 24:12b). Here we find the words "law" (*torah*) and "commandment" (*mitsvah*, singular) but not the word "covenant." Moses goes up with his assistant, Joshua, leaving Aaron and Hur at the foot of the mountain with the elders (vv. 13–14).

Having examined Exodus 24, the concluding chapter to the revelation of the Ten Commandments, we turn to the introductory chapter for further information. Like chapter 24, chapter 19 is a collage of sources. At times, the divine theophany (from the Greek for "appearance of God") seems like an earthquake and at times like a thunderstorm; at times the people are afraid to approach the mountain, and at other times they are drawn there and have to be restrained. The movements of Moses in Exodus 19 are confused (as we also saw in Exodus 24). Our concern, however, is with the understanding of covenant. The word appears only once, in verse 5: "Now therefore, if you obey my voice and keep my covenant [*berit*], you shall be my treasured possession out of all the peoples." To what covenant is God referring in this verse? The Sinai covenant has not been enacted yet, and the only stipulation in the Abrahamic covenant, circumcision of all males, is not unique to Israel (since Ishmael also keeps the covenant of circumcision). Scholars explain the confusion by reference to editing again. By noticing that the people's assent to the covenant in Exod 19:7 is identical to that in Exod 24:3 and virtually identical to Exod 24:7, we understand that this part of chapter 19 is deliberately composed as an introduction to the Ten Commandments.

As we discussed earlier, some scholars have discerned the suzerainty treaty as the organizing principle behind the "book of the covenant." If these scholars are correct, then the Exodus "book of the covenant" is missing some elements of the treaty format. In its current, edited form, the suzerain self-identifies as the LORD (Exod 19:3; 20:2) and provides a double historical prologue. Before the theophany, the LORD recites the threefold nature of the Israelite rescue: "You have seen what I did to the Egyptians, and how I bore you on eagles' wings and brought you to myself" (Exod 19:4). Immediately before the stipulations, a summary statement announces, "I am the LORD your God who brought you out of the land of Egypt, out of the house of slavery" (Exod 20:2). Stipulations occupy the text from Exod 20:3 to Exod 23:33. The stone tablets record some of the stipulations, and they are deposited in the ark for safekeeping and future reference. No witnesses are called, and no list of blessings and curses is detailed. This is not to say that the suzerainty treaty is not a part of the cultural backdrop that informs the "book of the covenant"— it is. But in its final form, the "book of the covenant" is not literarily structured so as to be readily recognized as a suzerainty treaty. Perhaps we are meant to understand that this covenant between God and God's people is both *like* the well-known suzerainty treaty and *unlike* it at the same time.

The "words" that God speaks in Exod 20:3–17 are repeated almost word for word in Deut 5:6–21. The only noticeable difference is in the Sabbath commandment. The Exodus version begins, "Remember," and grounds that remembrance in the seventh day of creation, when God took a Sabbath rest. The Deuteronomic version begins, "Observe," and gives as a warrant the rescue from slavery in Egypt. The Deuteronomic introduction is presented as a speech by Moses intended to remind the Israelites of all God has done so far on their behalf: "Hear, O Israel, the statutes and ordinances that I am addressing to you today; you shall learn them and observe them diligently. The LORD our God made a covenant [*berit*] with us at Horeb" (Deut 5:1b–2). We may also note language of covenant in Exodus 34. After Moses smashes the first set of stone tablets in anger over the golden calf incident, he is instructed to make a second set of tablets and come up the mountain to God. He obeys, and God declares in Exod 34:10, "I hereby make a covenant [*berit*]." What follows for the next sixteen verses are not the commandments from chapter 20 (although there are some similarities between these and what follows in chapter 34). At the end of this list in chapter 34, "The LORD said to Moses: Write these words; in accordance with these words I have made a covenant [*berit*] with you and with Israel. He was there with the LORD forty days and forty nights; he neither ate bread nor drank water. And he wrote on the tablets the words of the covenant [*berit*], the ten commandments [Hebrew: *words*]" (Exod 34:27–28). Note that even though the English says "ten commandments," the Hebrew says "ten words." Only three times are they specifically numbered as ten—here in Exod 34:28 and in Deut 4:13 and 10:4, where they are also called the "ten words." Moreover, the Old Testament in Hebrew *never* labels these verses the Ten Commandments. More often, biblical authors use a variety of words to refer to the divine stipulations. One need only look at Psalm 119 to marvel at the plethora of synonyms for "commandment." The standard language from Deuteronomy through Kings is "commandments, statutes, and ordinances." Only in postbiblical times did the title "Ten Commandments" become common parlance.

THE ARK OF THE COVENANT

We begin with some statistics about word usage. The ark is mentioned in the Old Testament approximately two hundred times—75 percent of the time simply as "the ark." Its importance in the biblical tradition is indicated by the sufficiency of simply saying "the ark." The Hebrew word is always 'aron, a word that means "chest," and is used almost exclusively to mean the ark of the covenant. (Once 'aron designates a coffin and a few times it means a money-chest; a different Hebrew word is used for Noah's ark.) The phrase "ark of the covenant" appears in the Old Testament fifty-five times, thirty-six times with an additional modifier, "of the LORD" or "of God." The Hebrew word berit is used forty-three times as the modifier of "the ark," especially in the writings attributed to the author(s) of Deuteronomy and the historical books. The Hebrew word 'edut is used twelve times (always in the Priestly source), nine times in Exodus, two times in Numbers, and one time in Joshua.

According to the tabernacle-building tradition in Exodus authored by the Priestly source, the ark was constructed by Bezalel, a craftsman from the tribe of Judah, who was called by God. The text affirms, "he [God] has filled him with divine spirit, with skill, intelligence, and knowledge in every kind of craft" (Exod 35:31). In Moses's version of events, he claims to have made the ark himself at the same time that he made the second set of stone tablets (Deut 10:3, 5). Almost four feet long and a little over two feet wide and high, the chest was easily portable by means of the poles on either side. Covered in gold, it must have been quite striking in the bright desert sunlight. The text describes two cherubim on top of the chest, with wings extended so that the tips touched in the center (Exod 37:7–9). Cherubim were winged creatures that combined features of beasts and humans, similar to the sphinx in Egypt or to the winged human-headed lions that protected doorways in Mesopotamia. Their function was to serve as guardians for the deity. The book of Exodus ends with an account of Moses's installation of the tabernacle and its furnishings: "He took the covenant [*'edut*] and put it into the ark, and put the poles on the ark, and set the mercy seat above the ark; and he brought the ark into the tabernacle, and set up the curtain for screening, and screened the ark of the covenant; as the LORD had commanded Moses" (Exod 40:20–21). Some have suggested, based on God's command to place the manna "before the LORD, to be kept throughout your generations" (Exod 16:33), that the ark also held a container of manna. Likewise the staff belonging to Aaron that produced almond buds has been supposed to have been in the ark, since it was to be placed "before the covenant [*'edut*]" (Num 17:10). The ark was understood to be a place of focused divine presence: "When Moses went into the tent of meeting to speak with the LORD, he would hear the voice speaking to him from above the mercy seat that was on the ark of the covenant from between the two cherubim; thus it spoke to him" (Num 7:89). This belief in the focused presence of the LORD was such that the ark led the army into battle (see, for example, Joshua 6, 1 Samuel 4). When the Philistines captured the ark in battle, such disasters came upon them that they eagerly sent it back to the Israelites (1 Samuel 5–6).

Before the temple was built in Jerusalem, the ark was apparently stationed at Bethel (Judg 20:27) and at Shiloh.

After David became king of Judah and Israel, he appropriately wished to have the ark of the covenant nearby. "David and all the people with him set out and went from Baale-judah, to bring up from there the ark of God, which is called by the name of the LORD of hosts who is enthroned on the cherubim" (2 Sam 6:2; see also 1 Sam 4:4). Then "they brought in the ark of the LORD, and set it in its place, inside the tent that David had pitched for it; and David offered burnt offerings and offerings of well-being before the LORD" (2 Sam 6:17). The task of building a permanent place for the ark would be left to David's successor, Solomon: "Then the priests brought the ark of the covenant of the LORD to its place, in the inner sanctuary of the house, in the most holy place, underneath the wings of the cherubim" (1 Kgs 8:6). Solomon announced to the assembly, "There I have provided a place for the ark, in which is the covenant of the LORD that he made with our ancestors when he brought them out of the land of Egypt" (1 Kgs 8:21). Mysteriously, this is the last Old Testament reference to the ark of the covenant in the temple. One other Old Testament verse enigmatically refers to the missing ark: "And when you have multiplied and increased in the land, in those days, says the LORD, they shall no longer say, 'The ark of the covenant of the LORD.' It shall not come to mind, or be remembered, or missed; nor shall another one be made" (Jer 3:16). Not one word exists in the biblical texts to explain what happened to the ark or when it disappeared from the temple.

God's Covenant with Phinehas

While most readers have felt on somewhat familiar ground with the discussions of Noah, Abraham, and Sinai, the average student of the Old Testament at this point is saying, "Phinehas? I've *never* heard of Phinehas! Who's he?" Granted, he is a minor character in the grand Old Testament narrative, but Phinehas is a party to a divine covenant and so deserves comment. He first appears in the genealogy in Exodus 6—readers may be excused from not studying genealogies—as the son of Putiel and Eleazar, and thus Aaron's grandson. Presumably he was anointed as a priest along with "Aaron and his sons" (Exod 40:12–15; Leviticus 8), although no names are given in these passages. We hear nothing more about him until Numbers 25, when he appears in the narrative as a zealous defender of the faith. Camped at Shittim, across the Jordan River from Jericho, the Israelite men engage in sexual relations with the women of the town. Variously designated as Moabite or Midianite, the women are specifically noted to be devotees to the local god, Baal of Peor (Num 25:1–3). When Phinehas sees that an Israelite man "brought a Midianite woman into his family, in the sight of Moses and in the sight of the whole congregation of the Israelites" (v 6), Phinehas responds with righteous indignation: "Taking a spear in his hand, he went after the Israelite man into the tent, and pierced the two of them, the Israelite and the woman, through the belly" (Num 25:7b–8), apparently catching them in the act. As Phinheas's reward, the LORD instructs Moses, "Therefore say, 'I hereby grant him my covenant [*berit*] of peace. It shall be for him and for his descendants after him a covenant [*berit*] of perpetual priesthood, because he was zealous for his God, and made atonement for the Israelites'" (Num 25:12–13). We can easily see the "grant covenant" background to the text. Coming from the Priestly source, this text that establishes the line of Aaron through Phinehas as priests in perpetuity is a helpful warrant for their service at the temple. Moreover, the very next chapter (Numbers 26) recounts the census taken in order to apportion the land of Canaan. Since priests are not given an allotment of property in the promised land, Phinehas's reward for zealotry cannot be the typical land grant. Rather, he is granted the right to a perpetual priesthood.

God's Covenant on the Plains of Moab

The book of Deuteronomy is, literarily speaking, the farewell address of Moses to the people of Israel. The first five verses of the book purport to pinpoint the geographic location of the Israelite camp. For our purposes, it is enough to know they are camped on the east side of the Jordan River toward the south, in the area broadly recognized as Moab. A sermonic introduction provides an extended self-identification of the God of Israel and a historical prologue of actions on behalf of these people. "Statutes and ordinances" occupy chapters 12–26, followed by a ritual ceremony and the listing of blessing and curses in chapters 27–28. The suzerainty treaty structure is apparent in the literary structure of Deuteronomy, although the hortatory nature of the introduction transforms the stipulations from legal compulsion to willing response.

Deuteronomy chapter 29 opens like this: "These are the words of the covenant [berit] that the LORD commanded Moses to make with the Israelites in the land of Moab, in addition to the covenant [*berit*] that he had made with them at Horeb" (Deut 29:1). (Deuteronomy prefers the name Horeb for the mountain otherwise known as Sinai.) The text specifically says that this covenant in the plains of Moab is *in addition to* the covenant at Sinai. We surmise that a new covenant is needed since the Israelites who were present at the original covenant at Sinai have all died in the wilderness (except Joshua and Caleb). In other words, this covenant making in Moab is the textual equivalent to passing on Abraham's covenant to Isaac and Jacob. Covering only two chapters, the Moab covenant manages to follow the suzerainty structure. After a self-identification and historical prologue (vv. 2–9), Moses urges everyone assembled "to enter into the covenant [*berit*] of the LORD your God, sworn by an oath, which the LORD your God is making with you today; in order that he may establish you today as his people, and that he may be your God, as he promised you and as he swore to your ancestors, to Abraham, to Isaac, and to Jacob" (Deut 29:12–13). The covenant is set under the umbrella of the Abrahamic covenant and uses the "code language" noted above. The stipulations are generalized into "observing all his commandments and decrees that are written in this book of the law" (Deut 30:10). Blessings will flow from following God; "following other gods" will bring about curses. Heaven and earth are called as witnesses to the covenant (Deut 30:19) since the typical ancient Near Eastern practice of summoning other gods as witnesses is clearly inappropriate.

God's Covenant with David

Most modern readers are back on familiar ground when we consider God's covenant with David—the promise that one of David's descendants will occupy the throne in perpetuity. The promise is first narrated in 2 Samuel 7, a literary jewel that revolves around word-play with the Hebrew word *bayit* ("house"). The word occurs eight times in the conversations between God and David, and between the prophet Nathan and David (vv. 1–17), and seven times in David's prayer of thanksgiving (vv. 18–29). Four different meanings are used for *bayit*: "palace" (house of the king), "temple" (house of God), "lineage"/"dynasty" (house of David), and "status" (household reputation). David wants to build God a house, but God declines and instead promises to build David a house. The core of the promise is in verses 13b–14a: "I will establish the throne of his [David's offspring] kingdom forever. I will be a father to him, and he shall be a son to me." Readers will recognize a variation of the covenant "code language": I will become God for you and you will become people for me.

The word *berit* is not mentioned at all in 2 Samuel 7; nowhere in the chapter is the promise to David characterized as a covenant. For that characterization, we have to turn to the poetic versions of the Davidic promise. Poetry is notoriously hard to date since concrete historical references are so rarely used. Poetic imagery deliberately lends itself to meaningful interpretation in any number of historical periods. All we can say for sure is that poetry referring to David and his covenant was composed sometime after David's reign (his reign is dated around approximately 1000 BCE). How much after, we cannot say.

Psalm 132 marries God's promise to David with God's selection of Zion as the divine habitation. The psalm is categorized as a "song of ascents" typically sung by pilgrims going up to Jerusalem. The poem begins with recollection of David's commitment to "find a place for the LORD, a dwelling place for the Mighty One of Jacob" (v. 5). Positioned in the poem as a reward is the promise to David: "The LORD swore to David a sure oath from which he will not turn back: 'One of the sons of your body I will set on your throne. If your sons keep my covenant [*berit*] and my decrees that I shall teach them, their sons also, forevermore, shall sit on your throne'" (vv. 11–12). Here the promise to David is termed "a sure oath." The reference to "covenant" is to the Sinai covenant. These verses could be understood as introducing conditionality into the Davidic promise: *if* the [Sinai] covenant is kept through the generations, then David's dynasty will continue past his immediate successor.

Psalm 89 contains more references to the Davidic promise. Categorized as "a maskil" (from the Hebrew root that means "be prudent, have insight"), the poem is attributed to Ethan the Ezrahite, who is mentioned as a wise man in 1 Kgs 4:31. In sum, the psalm recounts God's promise to David, laments that no Davidic king is currently on the throne, and petitions God to correct the situation. Since the Davidic promise is central to the psalmist's argument with God, we can mine the poem for theological insight into the Davidic covenant. The psalmist declares, "You said, 'I have made a covenant [*berit*] with my chosen one, I have sworn to my servant David: I will establish your descendants forever, and build your throne for all generations'" (vv. 3–4). Here is unambiguous confirmation that at least by the time of this psalm, the divine promise to David was understood to be a covenant. Moreover, it seems to be unconditional, that is, a grant covenant. Verses 19–37 describe the establishment of the covenant in greater detail, recalling God's words that "my covenant [*berit*] with him will stand firm" (v. 28b), and that "I will not violate my covenant [*berit*]" (v. 34). This section of the poem admits some conditionality, prescribing punishment if David's children "forsake my law" (vv. 30–32). But the conditionality is framed by statements of unconditionality: "I will establish his line forever, and his throne as long as the heavens endure" (v. 29); "His line shall continue forever, and his throne endure before me like the sun. It shall be established forever like the moon, an enduring witness in the skies" (vv. 36–37). In the end, readers have the idea that the divine intention is for a permanent Davidic presence on the throne; but in reality, human disobedience may make that intention impossible to fulfill.

Words attributed to David understand the promise as unambiguously unconditional and perpetual: "Is not my house like this with God? For he has made with me an everlasting covenant, ordered in all things and secure. Will he not cause to prosper all my help and my desire" (2 Sam 23:5)? The problem arises when what is understood as an unconditional, everlasting covenant is not manifest in reality. After 587 BCE no descendant from David's house sat on the throne; this situation raised the pressing problem of how to think about the Davidic covenant theologically. Two solutions emerged. In one, the covenant with David is universalized or democratized to all Israelites; a poem from the latter part of the exilic period adopts this solution: "I will make with you [plural, presumably the people of Israel] an everlasting covenant [*berit*], my steadfast, sure love for David" (Isa 55:3). The other solution is to push the Davidic royal expectations into the eschatological future. When God's reign comes in the fullness of the end times, then a king from the house of David will sit on the throne.

The Prophets

Finally we turn to the section of the Old Testament known as the prophets. In general, the prophets do not use the words *berit* or *'edut* explicitly to describe God's relationship with God's people. They do, however, criticize the people for behaviors that clearly violate the covenant relationship, and they exhort the people to live in ways that honor the covenant relationship. So the divine covenant is the backdrop for prophetic speech, whether explicitly acknowledged or not. Two notable exceptions are worthy of comment.

Ezekiel was active during the years that immediately preceded the exile to Babylon and into the first fifteen years of exile (approximately 593–563 BCE). In chapter 16 of the book that bears his name, the prophet accuses the people of unfaithfulness using an allegory of marriage (see also Hosea 1–3). God is portrayed as the husband who "pledged myself to you and entered into a covenant [*berit*] with you" (Ezek 16:8b). Then, using scathing vocabulary for fifty-eight verses, Ezekiel enumerates Israel's adulterous behavior, as the wife of the LORD God, and the deserved punishment. Remarkably, just when readers are totally convinced of the irredeemable nature of Israel, God says, "yet I will remember my covenant [*berit*] with you in the days of your youth, and I will establish with you an everlasting covenant [*berit*]" (Ezek 16:60). If ever readers doubted the grace-filled nature of God, this verse ends all theological depictions of God as a wrath-filled judge. One cannot help but be amazed by the grace of God to establish an everlasting covenant with such an undeserving group of people.

The other notable exception to silence about explicit covenant language in the prophetic literature is in the work attributed to the prophet Jeremiah. His prophecy is dated to the years just before Ezekiel, and much of his criticism of the people deals with their naïve belief that God's covenant with them will protect them from harm regardless of their behavior. Jeremiah's prophecies share similar themes and vocabulary with Deuteronomy, indicating that he was schooled in the traditions of Deuteronomy. For example,

> You shall say to them, Thus says the LORD, the God of Israel: Cursed be anyone who does not heed the words of this covenant [*berit*], which I commanded your ancestors when I brought them out of the land of Egypt, from the iron-smelter, saying, Listen to my voice, and do all that I command you. So shall you be my people, and I will be your God, that I may perform the oath that I swore to your ancestors, to give them a land flowing with milk and honey, as at this day. Then I answered, "So be it, LORD." (Jer 11:3–5)

After years of exhorting the people with little result, Jeremiah announces:

> The days are surely coming, says the LORD, when I will make a new covenant [*berit*] with the house of Israel and the house of Judah. It will not be

like the covenant that I made with their ancestors
when I took them by the hand to bring them out
of the land of Egypt—a covenant that they broke,
though I was their husband, says the LORD. But
this is the covenant that I will make with the
house of Israel after those days, says the LORD:
I will put my law [*torah*] within them, and I will
write it on their hearts; and I will be their God,
and they shall be my people. No longer shall they
teach one another, or say to each other, "Know the
LORD," for they shall all know me, from the least
of them to the greatest, says the LORD; for I will
forgive their iniquity, and remember their sin no
more. (Jer 31:31–34)

Readers will by now recognize the classic covenantal language here. But this is the only time in the Old
Testament that we encounter the adjective "new" with
berit. But readers should realize that all along we have
been encountering "new" covenants. Recall the explicit
language on the plains of Moab—that the covenant made
there is in addition to the one at Horeb/Sinai. What else is
that except "new"? The key theological question is, in what
sense is each covenant a new covenant? The Noah covenant was between God and all living things. When God
cut a covenant with Abraham (literally), it could certainly
be described as new; the promise of land and descendants
are new, and the sign of circumcision is new. But nowhere
does the biblical tradition understand the covenant with
Abraham as nullifying the covenant with Noah. In fact,
even as late (biblically speaking) as the mid-first century
CE, the prohibition from the Noah covenant against eating meat with blood is the basis of dietary laws for the
Gentiles (Acts 15:19–20). The Sinai covenant is new, since

it enjoins on the people rescued from Egypt a whole series of statutes and ordinances. But again, nowhere does the biblical tradition understand the Sinai covenant as nullifying the Abrahamic covenant. In fact, in most of the biblical tradition, the two are referenced together (see, for example, Jer 11:3–5), as if the Sinai covenant supplements the Abrahamic covenant. The promise of land and descendants endures, but the stipulations are expanded from only circumcision to a whole range of regulations for community life. We noted above that the covenant on the plains of Moab, while in addition to the Sinai covenant, does not negate it. David's covenant is new, since it establishes a particular lineage as the legitimate royal dynasty. But again, the Davidic covenant does not nullify the Sinai covenant; in fact the length of the king's reign depends on obedience to the Sinai covenant: "When he has taken the throne of his kingdom, he shall have a copy of this law [*torah*] written for him in the presence of the Levitical priests. It shall remain with him and he shall read in it all the days of his life, so that he may learn to fear the LORD his God, diligently observing all the words of this law and these statutes, neither exalting himself above other members of the community nor turning aside from the commandment, either to the right or to the left, so that he and his descendants may reign long over his kingdom in Israel" (Deut 17:18–20). The evidence is clear that when Jeremiah characterizes the covenant as "new," he does not mean that it nullifies earlier covenants. Its newness derives from the interiority of the covenant: it is written on hearts so that every person has immediate access to the divine intention for abundant life. The natural trajectory of this line of thought is to assert that when Jesus announces "the new covenant in my blood" (Luke 22:20; 1 Cor 11:25), biblical tradition does not permit an understanding that nullifies the previous covenants. Its newness is in the person and mission of Jesus of Nazareth, whom God sent to yet again invite people into a covenant relationship so that "I will become God for them and they will become people for me."

THREE

Cultus

IN THIS CHAPTER WE explore ancient Israelite worship rituals and theology, what scholars call the *cultus* or *cult*. Unfortunately, the word *cult* conjures up images in the modern readers' minds of bizarre rituals, brainwashing, and charismatic leaders like Charles Manson, David Koresh, or Sun Jung Moon. In modern parlance, a cult is unorthodox, regarded with suspicion, and shunned by the mainstream religious authorities. In the ancient world, a cult—more precisely, *the* cult—was the exact opposite: orthodox, suspicious of any rival theology or practice, and supported and staffed by mainstream religious authorities. The English word derives from Latin roots where it means "care" or "adoration." We begin by examining biblical texts describing the orthodox cult in ancient Israel—the temple, the priests, and the rituals of sacrifice. Then we "read between the lines" to tease out the unorthodox rituals and theology operative alongside the orthodox cult.

STRUCTURES FOR THE CULT

The complex literary history of the texts of the Old Testament precludes a facile reading that unquestioningly identifies any ritualistic structure described in the text to the time period described in the text. Nevertheless, the texts outline a trajectory in places of worship from local to centralized, from outside to inside, from easily accessible to inaccessible.

Altar

The word *altar* appears about four hundred times in the Old Testament across twenty-five of the thirty-nine books. In texts describing cultic life prior to the temple in Jerusalem, the altar seems to be the primary cultic structure. The Hebrew word *mizbeach* means literally, "sacrifice-place," indicating the primary cultic purpose of the altar (the Hebrew consonants *z-b-ch* mean "to sacrifice"). Altars were "built," "made," or "erected" from soil, wood, or stone. Early texts connect building altars with the divine presence. Abram leaves Haran and journeys to Shechem, approximately midway through the land of Canaan: "Then the LORD appeared to Abram, and said, 'To your offspring I will give this land.' So he built there an altar to the LORD, who had appeared to him. From there he moved on to the hill country on the east of Bethel, and pitched his tent, with Bethel on the west and Ai on the east; and there he built an altar to the LORD and invoked the name of the LORD" (Gen 12:7–8). Apparently, Abram built an altar first out of gratitude for the divine promise of descendants and then in order to call upon the LORD for continued blessing and protection. Later, Abram settled by Hebron and built another altar there (Gen 13:18). The best-known altar built by Abram was for the explicit purpose of sacrificing the child of the promise (Gen 22:9). Abraham's son Isaac built an altar at Beersheba to commemorate the divine appearance (Gen 26:25). Abraham's grandson Jacob built altars at

Shechem and at Bethel: "Then come, let us go up to Bethel, that I may make an altar there to the God who answered me in the day of my distress and has been with me wherever I have gone" (Gen 35:3). In none of these accounts do we hear about any explicit activity at the altar; the altar appears in the text as a memorial structure more than a place of sacrifice (except for Abraham's near sacrifice of Isaac). In other texts, stone pillars serve as memorials, sometimes anointed with oil to mark them as holy (see, for example, Genesis 28).

In contrast to the texts just mentioned, other texts about altars describe the sacrificial activity that took place there. Upon disembarking from the ark, Noah built an altar and offered whole burnt offerings to the LORD, the pleasant odor of which caused the LORD to relent from further destruction (Gen 8:20–21). In the composite chapter concluding the episode in which God reveals the Ten Commandments and other laws at Mt. Sinai, Moses built an altar, and the young men "offered burnt offerings and sacrificed oxen as offerings of well-being to the LORD" (Exod 24:5). Moses dashed blood against the altar and over the assembly (Exod 24:6–8). Gideon built an altar to the LORD after being assured of victory in the upcoming battle with the Midianites and offered up his father's second bull (Judg 6:26).

The purpose of the altar as a sacrifice-place is explicit in the laws that follow the Ten Commandments: "You need make for me only an altar of earth and sacrifice on it your burnt offerings and your offerings of well-being, your sheep and your oxen; in every place where I cause my name to be remembered I will come to you and bless you. But if you make for me an altar of stone, do not build it of hewn stones; for if you use a chisel upon it you profane it. You shall not go up by steps to my altar, so that your nakedness may not be exposed on it" (Exod 20:24–26). These instructions probably provide a visual distinction between Israelite altars and Canaanite altars. The phrase "where I cause my name to be remembered" is typical of language in Deuteronomy, which is concerned with the distinctiveness of the Israelites from the Canaanites and other West Semitic peoples.

A few texts indicate that altars had horns on the four corners, perhaps originally rams' horns but later constructed of the same material as the altar itself: "He made the altar of incense of acacia wood, one cubit long, and one cubit wide; it was square, and was two cubits high; its horns were of one piece with it" (Exod 37:25). When the horned altar needed to be set apart as a sacrifice-place, blood was daubed on the four horns to sanctify it (Exod 29:12; Leviticus 4). Apparently, grasping hold of the horns of the altar was a way of claiming sanctuary: "Solomon was informed, 'Adonijah is afraid of King Solomon; see, he has laid hold of the horns of the altar, saying, "Let King Solomon swear to me first that he will not kill his servant with the sword"'" (1 Kgs 1:51).

Tabernacle

According to the biblical narrative, the people construct an elaborate cultic structure in the wilderness for the divine presence. The Hebrew word for this structure is *mishkan*, literally "dwelling-place" (the Hebrew root *sh-k-n* means "to dwell"). This Hebrew root will later be utilized in Greek to mean "dwell," most notably in John 1:14: "And the Word became flesh and lived [*s-k-n*] among us, and we have seen his glory, the glory as of a father's only son, full of grace and truth." Later Jewish mystics would name the divine presence the *Shekinah*, also derived from this root. Thirteen chapters in Exodus are devoted to the tabernacle structure, seven to its design (chaps. 25–31) and six to its construction (chaps. 35–40). Sandwiched between these detailed accounts are the incident with the golden calf and the gracious divine recommitment to the people. Moses first receives the command to build the tabernacle when he is on top of Mount Sinai:

> The LORD said to Moses: Tell the Israelites to take for me an offering; from all whose hearts prompt them to give you shall receive the offering for me. This is the offering that you shall receive from them: gold, silver, and bronze, blue, purple, and crimson yarns and fine linen, goats' hair, tanned rams' skins, fine leather, acacia wood, oil for the lamps, spices for the anointing oil and for the fragrant incense, onyx stones and gems to be set in the ephod and for the breastpiece. And have them make me a sanctuary [*miqdash*], so that I may dwell among them. In accordance with all that I show you concerning the pattern of the tabernacle [*mishkan*] and of all its furniture, so you shall make it. (Exod 25:1–9)

The range of gifts specified—precious metals, textiles, wood, oil, and stone—makes it immediately obvious that this is a shrine of a far different character from a simple altar. In fact, the altar will only be one small part of this grand structure. This tabernacle will be the dwelling place of the divine, constructed of precious materials worthy of the divine presence. Moreover, the dwelling place will be divinely designed, not unlike the universe itself. The architectural blueprint is given to Moses in excruciating detail for three chapters: the ark containing the testimony (*'edut*) (Exod 25:10–22); the table for the bread of the Presence (Exod 25:23–30); the seven-branched candelabra (Exod 25:31–40); curtains, veil, and screen for the tabernacle (Exod 26:1–6, 15–37); curtains for the tent over the tabernacle (Exod 26:7–14); altar and utensils for burnt offerings (Exod 27:1–8); court enclosure hangings (Exod 27:9–19); and lamp (Exod 27:20–21). The next four chapters detail the rituals to take place at the tabernacle (considered below): priestly vestments (Exod 28:1–43); ordination rituals (Exod 29:1–37); daily burnt offerings (Exod 29:38–46); incense altar (Exod 30:1–10); ransom rituals (Exod 30:11–16); laver (Exod 30:17–21); anointing rituals (Exod 30:22–38); and appointment of craftsmen (Exod 31:1–11). Organized from the most interior space to the outer courtyard and from the most sacred furnishings to the most accessible, the divine blueprint describes a portable sanctuary for the divine presence to go with the people on the move toward the promised land. The narration of the construction of the tabernacle is no less detailed, as the people bring the divine blueprint to life. These tabernacle sections in Exodus (description and construction) are similar to the ancient Mesopotamian practice called *ishkaru*, in which temple craftsmen must account in detail for the use of raw materials in their finished products.

Again, note the complex literary history of the biblical texts, whereby certain texts that appear early in the biblical narrative are actually late literary compositions. Such is the case with the tabernacle chapters. Despite the biblical notation that the Israelites plundered the Egyptians upon leaving Egypt, it is impossible that the freed slaves in the wilderness would have had the materials specified in the tabernacle narrative. Described as an elaborate, portable tent-shrine, the tabernacle is probably a retrojection from a later period, either an elaborate tent-shrine in Shiloh after the settlement in Canaan or a fictive picture based on the Jerusalem temple. The rationale of the biblical authors and editors might have gone something like this: "We don't have any living witnesses to what the wilderness tabernacle looked like, but it must have been a grand structure. After all, our Israelite ancestors were celebrating their liberation from generations of slavery and would have contributed their most precious materials to the construction effort. Besides, we know that the tabernacle was divinely designed—every deity designs his own temple—and a divinely designed worship space must have been glorious in every respect." This is not to say that some sort of portable tent structure for the ark of the covenant did not exist in the wilderness, only that the Exodus account exaggerates its extravagance.

But the "accuracy" of the description of the tabernacle is not the point of the narrative. The point is theological: God has committed to dwell with this people on their journey to inhabit the land of promise. With a portable dwelling-place, God can never lose this people, no matter where they roam or how far they stray.

Temple

Modern readers may be surprised to learn there is no specific Hebrew word for "temple." Given the temple's prominence in the biblical texts, we would expect an exclusive use of a particular Hebrew word: something like what we mean in English by using "Temple" with a capital *T*. There is no such exclusive word. The temple is regularly called a "house" in the Old Testament: "house of the LORD" (*bet-YHWH*) or "house of God" (*bet-'el* or *bet-'elohim*) or simply the "house" (*bayit*) for short. "House" is *bayit* and "house of" is *bet*; readers may be interested to know that Hebrew *bet* is frequently transliterated as *beth*, yielding the familiar place names Beth-lehem ("house of bread") and Beth-el ("house of God"). The use of the common word for "house" is in keeping with traditions throughout the ancient Near East, where temples of the various deities were called, for instance, the "house of Ishtar" in Mesopotamia or "house of Dagon" in Philistia (see, for example, 1 Sam 5:2). This usage depicts the common ancient belief that the deity took up residence in the house constructed for him or her, not in a literal sense as humans take up residence in a house, but in a metaphorical sense. The house of the god was the place where one could be assured of the divine presence; similarly, modern worshipers may feel assurance of God's presence in the sanctuary of a church, mosque, or synagogue. None of us believes that God actually lives there, but we affirm God's promise to be especially present in that place.

The other Hebrew word used commonly in connection with a temple is *hekal*. The word probably came into Hebrew from the ancient Mesopotamian words *ekallu* and

É.GAL, meaning "great house." When the resident of the "great house" is the king, the English translations render the Hebrew word as "palace," and when the resident is the deity, the English translation is "temple." When the two common Hebrew words *bayit* and *hekal* are used together in reference to the temple, usually *bayit* or *bet* refers to the overall structure, and *hekal* refers to the enclosed space behind the altar.

Throughout the ancient Near East, the responsibility for constructing the house of the deity fell to the king. In addition to securing the nation's borders with armies and securing the nation's dynastic reign with sons, the king needed to secure the nation's prosperity with residences for the gods. Securing the divine presence by building temples was a fundamental responsibility of the king, about which the king boasted to neighboring nations and to future generations. Materials and labor were provided by the king, whether from personal resources or from additional exaction from the populace. At the completion of the temple, the king dedicated the temple to the god, positioning his selection as builder as confirmation of his selection as national ruler. When a new king assumed the throne, if new construction was impractical, then renovations, refurbishment, or increased cultic activity served to confirm the god's selection.

As was discussed in chapter 2, the authors and editors of the Old Testament understood that God had selected David and his sons in an everlasting covenant to serve as royal rulers. Similarly, in the final form of the biblical texts, God selected a particular place in which to dwell: Jerusalem or Zion. Mountains were typically associated with earthly residences for the divine in the ancient world, no doubt because they seemed to reach into the heavens, the real dwelling place of the gods. Early Mesopotamian temples mimicked the shape of mountains with the ziggurat, a stepped pyramid-shaped constructed of mud bricks. Jerusalem, atop a mountainous ridge in Judah at more than twenty-five hundred feet above sea level, is a natural location for the Temple (with a capital *T*) that will serve as the residence for Israel's God. In the biblical texts, Zion is used both for the area also known as Jerusalem and for the specific mountain site of the temple. One of the central tenets of the book of Deuteronomy is that God has chosen one site as the centralized site for cultic activity in the promised land. Written from the geographic perspective of the people's being poised outside the promised land anticipating entrance, the author of Deuteronomy places in Moses's mouth this command: "But you shall seek the place that the LORD your God will choose out of all your tribes as his habitation to put his name there" (Deut 12:5). Careful not to specify the exact location, the text calls for trust in God, who has accompanied them thus far. Even though the postexilic Deuteronomic editors know that the selection is Jerusalem, their leaving the location ambiguous in the text reinforces the theological belief that the place of cultic activity is God's choice, not the people's choice. After the people had entered the land and constructed the temple, the biblical authors reflect: "For the LORD has chosen Zion; he has desired it for his habitation: 'This is my resting place forever; here I will reside, for I have desired it'" (Ps 132:13–14).

According to the biblical narrative, King David decided the time had come to build a permanent structure for the ark of the covenant as a replacement for the current tent shrine. This is totally in keeping with his royal responsibility: borders were secure since "the LORD had given him rest from all his enemies around him" (2 Sam 7:1); royal lineage had been secured since "sons were born to David at Hebron" (2 Sam 3:1). Securing the divine presence, therefore, was the next major task for King David. The anomaly, of course, is that David does *not* build the temple. Different biblical voices make theological sense of this "problem" in various ways. The "majority" voice in the Samuel-Kings narrative delays the building until the reign of David's son Solomon. When David announces his intentions to the prophet Nathan, God tells David through Nathan that no permanent residence is necessary: "Wherever I have moved about among all the people of Israel, did I ever speak a word with any of the tribal leaders of Israel, whom I commanded to shepherd my people Israel, saying, 'Why have you not built me a house of cedar?'" (2 Sam 7:7). The point seems to be that David has initiated the building project, not God. Rather, as part of the covenant with David, God assures David that his son will build the temple. Interestingly, in direct contradiction to peaceful conditions reported in 2 Sam 7:1, King Solomon reports to King Hiram of Tyre: "You know that my father David could not build a house for the name of the LORD his God because of the warfare with which his enemies surrounded him, until the LORD put them under the soles of his feet" (1 Kgs 5:3).

A different reason is given by the Chronicler, the name given to the anonymous author of Chronicles, Ezra, and Nehemiah, written in the second half of the first millennium BCE. In this version of events, King David explains to his son Solomon, "My son, I had planned to build a house to the name of the LORD my God. But the word of the LORD came to me, saying, 'You have shed much blood and have waged great wars; you shall not build a house to my name, because you have shed so much blood in my sight on the earth'" (1 Chr 22:7–8). If shedding blood excluded kings from building temples in the ancient Near East, no temples would have been built at all! Even though the actual construction is left to Solomon, in the Chronicler's account David makes all the preparations of materials and leaves explicit, detailed instructions for leaders and cultic activities. Solomon is simply the automaton who carries out David's orders: this telling meets an important theological objective for the Chronicler's work—to show the importance of David in the religious life of Israel.

What did the Jerusalem temple look like? The only available record is the building account in 1 Kings 6–7; no independent archives have yet surfaced to confirm or deny the biblical description. Unlike the in the tabernacle account, there is no description of a divine blueprint for the temple. Solomon apparently built a structure that resembled other temples in Syria-Palestine. According to the biblical text, the Jerusalem temple was a rectangular structure approximately ninety feet long by thirty feet wide, constructed of hewn stone. The inside walls were paneled in cedar from Lebanon, and the floor was paneled in cypress—also imported from the north. Carvings of cherubim and palm flowers decorated the cedar paneling, which was also adorned with gold leaf. Three stories of storage chambers were located on three sides. Only a small section was enclosed; most of the temple was open-air. Two freestanding bronze columns twenty-four feet high and eighteen feet in circumference were erected in

the outermost courtyard and named *Jachin* ("God establishes") and *Boaz* ("he comes with power"). Located also
in the courtyard was a huge bronze bowl fifteen feet in
diameter, seven and a half feet deep, and forty-five feet
in circumference, with a capacity of about twelve thousand gallons of water. This "molten sea" was supported
on the hindquarters of twelve oxen facing outward, with
three facing each compass direction. On the north and
south sides of the enclosed area were ten smaller bronze
basins (with a total capacity of about two hundred forty
gallons) supported by bronze stands designed as wagons
and decorated with cherubim, lions, and palm trees. The
outer courtyard also contained the altar for burnt offerings. Separated from the outer courtyard by doors, the
nave contained the golden altar for burning incense, the
table for the bread of the presence, and ten lampstands,
each topped with a small bowl and wick for burning oil.
The innermost chamber was separated from the nave by
another set of doors. Here in the "Holy of Holies" the ark
of the covenant was stationed. The biblical text narrates
a seven-day dedicatory celebration in which "Solomon offered as sacrifices of well-being to the LORD twenty-two
thousand oxen and one hundred twenty thousand sheep"
(1 Kgs 8:63). Afterwards, "the LORD appeared to Solomon
a second time . . . 'I have consecrated this house that you
have built, and put my name there forever; my eyes and
my heart will be there for all time'" (1 Kgs 9:2–3). The implications would have been obvious to the ancient hearer:
appropriate sacrifice guarantees the divine presence.

This magnificent structure would be razed to the
ground and burned by the armies of King Nebuchadnezzar
in 587 BCE. The bronze pillars and molten sea were disas-

sembled for transport to Babylon, along with all the temple implements and utensils. The place known as Zion, God's chosen habitation, would remain vacant until the second Jerusalem temple was constructed on the same spot and dedicated in 515 BCE on "the third day of the month of Adar, in the sixth year of the reign of King Darius [of Persia]" (Ezra 6:15). Oddly, the Bible gives no account of the building of the Second temple comparable to the extensive texts describing the erection of the tabernacle or of the first Jerusalem temple—only brief and conflicting descriptions of the multiple attempts to reconstruct the temple appear. We surmise that the second temple reconstructed with a roughly similar design to the architectural design of the first temple.

Whatever the second temple looked like, Herod the Great undertook an extensive expansion of it in the final decades of the first millennium. "Herod's temple" is the one most familiar to modern readers, since a scale model is on exhibit in the Israel Museum, and actual ancient stones are visible on the Temple Mount in present-day Jerusalem.

WORKERS IN THE CULT

Even as readers must untangle various threads in the biblical texts to imagine the ancient cultic structures, multiple texts describe the workers in the cult in various ways. Archives of temple texts in ancient Mesopotamia, Egypt, and Greece have illumined our understanding of temple activity in the ancient Near East. Although no such temple archives have yet been excavated for the Jerusalem temple, we may fairly assume that the Jerusalem cult operated in many of the same ways as other cults. Temple cults were supported by large numbers of workers in multiple fields of service. In this section, we will divide the discussion into two main categories: priests and others. By *priests*, we mean those personnel who were charged with the day-to-day activity directly related to assuring the divine presence. By *others*, we mean those who made it possible for the priests to do their work.

Priests

The most frequent Hebrew word for "priest" is *kohen*, a word from which many modern readers will recognize the derivative Jewish surname Cohen. We may think of the *kohen* as the ritual specialist, the one designated by the deity and acknowledged by the community as being set apart for divine service. The modern analog would be pastor, rabbi, or imam. In the ancient world, being a priest was a family affair, since heredity was the primary qualification. Typically, one was born into the priestly profession, so the biblical texts can refer to "the sons of Aaron" or "Levites" (meaning those born into the tribe of Levi). But priesthood was not an inalienable birthright, since inappropriate behavior could cause the disenfranchisement of priests. For example, fire consumed two sons of Aaron when "they offered unholy fire before the LORD, such as he had not commanded them" (Lev 10:1). The two sons of Eli, the priests at Shiloh, were condemned to death by God because "they treated the offerings of the LORD with contempt" (1 Sam 2:17). On the other hand, the story of the young Samuel demonstrates that boys from nonpriestly families could be donated to the priesthood (1 Samuel 1). Although Samuel is never actually called a *kohen*, he performs all the duties of a *kohen*: offering sacrifices, performing divination, making intercessory prayers, and anointing kings. And there is the strange story of a young man serving a shrine, whose lineage is specifically given as "from the clan of Judah," yet at the same time he is called a Levite (Judg 17:7). Apparently the term *Levite* here is a vocational term and not a designation of lineage.

The biblical texts give the overall impression that two categories of priests operated in ancient Israel. The texts seem to indicate that the some priests performed the most sacred rituals, leaving the more mundane or routine tasks for another category of priests. The story of the birth of Moses begins, "Now a man from the house of Levi went and married a Levite woman," (Exod 2:1), setting up indisputable Levitical credentials for Moses. Levi, the third son of Jacob and Leah, is extolled as the one who serves as a priest in the poetic farewell blessing of Moses (Deut 33:8). Aaron is first mentioned in the biblical story when Moses begs God to send someone else on this foolhardy mission to liberate the Israelite slaves from bondage in Egypt: "Then the anger of the LORD was kindled against Moses and he said, 'What of your brother Aaron, the Levite? I know that he can speak fluently; even now he is coming out to meet you, and when he sees you his heart will be glad'" (Exod 4:14). The genealogy of Levi in Exod 6:16–25 traces to Aaron and Moses, and then continues tracing the line only through Aaron. Priests who could prove they were direct descendants of Aaron eventually succeeded in upstaging other descendants in the line of Levi, with the result that the Aaronide priests can be referred to in biblical texts as just "priests," whereas the others are called either "Levitical priests" or "Levites."

This struggle for preeminence between descendants of Aaron and other descendants of Levi apparently lasted over several centuries and left traces in the biblical texts. On the one hand, certain texts are clearly pro-Levite (favoring non-Aaronide descendants): for example, the golden calf incident and its aftermath. The narrative ascribes fault for the apostasy of the golden calf primarily to Aaron, and he comes off as a sucker and a liar. The people are impatient and persuade him to fashion the image of a bull from their donated gold pieces. When confronted by Moses, he disavows any responsibility: "I threw it [the gold] into the fire, and out came this calf!" (Exod 32:24b). Moses summons the "sons of Levi" who circulate among the offenders with swords, killing "about three thousand." Moses says, "Today you have ordained yourselves for the service of the LORD, each one at the cost of a son or a brother, and so have brought a blessing on yourselves this day" (Exod 32:29). On the other hand, certain texts clearly support the subordination of the Levite priests to the Aaronide priests. For example, "You shall give the Levites to Aaron and his descendants; they are unreservedly given to him from among the Israelites" (Num 3:9), and "Thereafter the Levites went in to do their service in the tent of meeting in attendance on Aaron and his sons" (Num 8:22).

During David's reign, two chief priests were appointed: Zadok, an Aaronide priest, and Ahimelech, a Levitical priest (non-Aaronide). Perhaps David's political acumen persuaded him to share priestly power rather than choose one lineage over another. Solomon later banished the non-Aaronide, Levitical priests from the temple, retaining only the Aaronide family of Zadok as priests. Some texts indicate that the Levitical priests continued to hold sway in the northern parts of Israel until its fall in 721 BCE. Many scholars posit that the Levites may have been the authors of the book of Deuteronomy. The literary center of the book of Deuteronomy declares the divine choice of the Levites: "For the LORD your God has chosen Levi out of all your tribes, to stand and minister in the name of the LORD, him and his sons for all time" (Deut 18:5). By the time of the final editing and compiling of the Pentateuch, the Aaronide priests were in charge of the Levitical priests, and this situation resulted in the overall impression of Aaronide superiority from the beginning. The Aaronide priests are the ones scholars mean by the Priestly source, the final editors of the Pentateuch. The book of Leviticus is almost entirely about the Aaronide priests, even though the title clearly derives from the word *Levite*.

By the time the official position of "chief priest" developed at the temple, the descendants of Zadok, of the line of Aaron, were in full control. The Zadokites, as they were known in Hebrew, are called the Sadducees in Greek. The Sadducees in the New Testament are the Jewish sect most concerned with priestly ritual, even if accommodation to the Roman overlords is the price to be paid to maintain temple ritual.

Others

In the large temple estates of Mesopotamia, hundreds of workers were needed to perform the daily duties associated with the cult. Most temples contained at least one small statue of the god to whom the temple was dedicated, symbolizing the god's presence on earth. Lest modern readers disparage ancient ritualists as stupid (or worse), we should be clear: the ancients understood their actions as symbolic. Everyone knew that the god's real residence was in heaven; attending to the cult statue was a way of focusing human attention on the otherwise-unknowable divine presence. According to texts found in temple archives, these cult statues were routinely treated as royal personages, that is, offered meals several times a day, bathed and clothed, and taken out for "walks." Skilled artisans in gold and other precious metals crafted the cult statues and the decorative jewelry to adorn the statue. Meals offered to the cult statues required millers and bakers to turn high-quality flour into breads, porridges, and sweet cakes. Soakers prepared dates for use in baking, and pressers extracted oil from sesame. Accompanying the meals were libations of beer or wine, requiring brewers and vintners. Supporting personnel in the food and drink preparation included measurers, sweepers, fuel suppliers, and porters. The cult statue was clothed in fine garments of wool or linen. Expert weavers were needed along with dyers and cutters of reeds, used to stir the cloth in the dye and as fuel for the dyeing chemicals. Washers, bleachers, fullers, and menders dealt with what the ancient texts refer to as "dirty linen." Goat hair was used to weave the many sacks that were needed to hold the produce coming into the temple storehouses. Weavers were supported by water-drawers, measurers, and porters.

In addition to skilled craftsmen, the large temple estates needed hundreds of farmers and herders to maintain the cultivation acres and herds that supplied the temple's needs. Agricultural tools and implements for the herds were crafted by carpenters, smiths, and leatherworkers. (Necessary implements included, e.g., spades, shovels, sickles, axes, plowshares, bridles, yokes knives, shearing clippers, wagon wheels, quivers, and arrows.) Ironsmiths were busy fashioning nails, rings for doors, censers, bowls, and other vessels needed throughout the temple complex. Carpenters built furniture, litters, and ships to be used in processions. Reeds needed to be soaked, peeled, and bleached to weave into baskets and mats. Animal hides were converted into parchment by leatherworkers. And, of course, administrative personnel were needed to keep track of inventories, to record items coming into and out of the temple storehouses, to pay rations and/or wages to workers, to settle disputes, and the like.

As we have said before, since no temple archives have yet been excavated from the Jerusalem temple, the biblical texts remain our only source of information. Scholars debate the extent of the Jerusalem temple's landholdings and, therefore, the extent of its personnel. Biblical texts specifically mention various types of musicians, usually noted as Levites, as well as gatekeepers. I have argued in another book that the Hebrew word *sho'er* is mistranslated in English versions as "gatekeeper." The position was likely a gate accountant, charged with collecting tithes and offerings from persons passing through the gates of the temple, assaying the items, assigning value, and crediting the person's temple account.

CHARACTERISTICS OF THE CULT

Two features of the Israelite cult distinguish it from virtually all other cults of the ancient Near East. However much ancient Israel was heir and participant in the surrounding cultures, the orthodox cult of ancient Israel was distinctive from surrounding cultures in two important ways.

First, the Israelite cult was exclusive, devoted only to the God of Israel. Today, we call such exclusiveness monotheism, the theological doctrine of only (*mono*) one god (*theos*). Some biblical texts may be cited to support exclusive monotheism in ancient Israel—most notably, those from Second Isaiah. For example, "I am the LORD, and there is no other; besides me there is no god" (Isa 45:5; see also v. 18b). But we may also read these texts as trying to persuade the ancient hearers that the God of Israel is unequaled in power; that is, there is no other god who can save them from their current distressful situation. For example, also from Second Isaiah: "I, I am the LORD, and besides me there is no savior" (Isa 43:11). Most likely, ancient Israel was not monotheistic per se during the time of the writings of the Old Testament. Rather, Israel was henotheistic—from the Greek words for "one" (*hen*) and "god" (*theos*). Whereas strict monotheism acknowledges the existence of only one god, henotheism may acknowledge the existence of multiple gods but calls for the worship of only one god. That is, we may construct a theological trajectory from polytheism (many gods exist and are worshiped) to henotheism (many gods exist, and one is worshiped) to monotheism (only one God exists and is worshiped). Many Old Testament texts acknowledge the existence of other deities; the difference, succinctly formulated in the First Commandment, is that Israel is to *worship* only one deity: "you shall have no other gods before me" (Exod 20:3). The cult is to be exclusively devoted to the God of Israel alone. This seemingly simple reality was to be a constant snare for ancient Israel, living in the midst of polytheistic cultures (see below). The covenant ceremony at Shechem recounted in Joshua 24 puts the choice starkly:

> "Now therefore revere the LORD, and serve him in sincerity and in faithfulness; put away the gods that your ancestors served beyond the River and in Egypt, and serve the LORD. Now if you are unwilling to serve the LORD, choose this day whom you will serve, whether the gods your ancestors served in the region beyond the River or the gods of the Amorites in whose land you are living; but as for me and my household, we will serve the LORD." Then the people answered, "Far be it from us that we should forsake the LORD to serve other gods." (Josh 24:14–16a)

God's demand for exclusive worship earns the adjective *jealous* in the biblical texts: "for you shall worship no other god, because the LORD, whose name is Jealous, is a jealous God" (Exod 34:14); "For the LORD your God is a devouring fire, a jealous God" (Deut 4:24). God's jealousy is aroused when God's people worship another god, igniting God's wrath and resulting in the people's punishment. The Hebrew verb most frequently associated with the attitude of exclusive worship is "love"; to "love the LORD your God with all your heart, and with all your soul, and with all your might" (Deut 6:5) means to be bound to God exclusively in covenant relationship and is expressed by exclusive worship and obedience.

The Israelite cult was not only exclusive. Second, it was aniconic, that is, it allowed no image of the deity. Whereas cults in other areas cared for cult statues, no such statues were permitted in the orthodox Israelite cult (but see below for unorthodox practices). This prohibition resounds through all genres of biblical literature: law, historical narrative, prophetic oracle, and poetic meditation. Several Hebrew words are used in connection with the prohibition of images. A generic word for image is *tselem*, possibly related to the Assyrian and Arabic words that mean "cut off." This is the word used in Gen 1:27 to describe humankind made in the image of God. Literally, humanity is a chip off the divine block. The Hebrew *pesel* comes from the verb that means "to hew into shape" and can refer to an image made from stone, wood, or metal. Similarly, the Hebrew verb "to shape or fashion" yields the Hebrew noun *'atsab*, "something fashioned," usually in connection with silver or gold. Hebrew *massekah*, from the verb "to pour out," refers specifically to a cast or molten image. The Hebrew *gillul* comes from the verb "to roll" and apparently refers to images made from logs. The generic word translated "idols" in English is frequently the Hebrew word *'elil*: literally, "worthless thing."

The first prohibition against images in the canon is near the beginning of the Ten Commandments, part of the first paragraph in the Hebrew text, but numbered as the second commandment for Jews and Reformed Christians: "You shall not make for yourself an idol [*pesel*], whether in the form of anything that is in heaven above, or that is on the earth beneath, or that is in the water under the earth" (Exod 20:4). This prohibition is repeated numerous times throughout the Pentateuch (see, for example, Exod 34:17; Lev 19:4; Deut 4:23). The historical narratives frequently evaluate kings as evil because they make cultic images. For example, because King Jeroboam I set up two golden calves in temples in Dan and Bethel, he is condemned to be eaten by dogs since "you have done evil above all those who were before you and have gone and made for yourself other gods, and cast images [*massekah*], provoking me to anger, and have thrust me behind your back" (1 Kgs 14:9); King Ahab is condemned because "he acted most abominably in going after idols [*gillul*], as the Amorites had done, whom the LORD drove out before the Israelites" (1 Kgs 21:26); under King Hoshea, "they [the people of Israel] served idols [*gillul*], of which the LORD had said to them, 'You shall not do this'" (2 Kgs 17:12).

The psalmists incorporate the prohibition against images into their poems:

- "All worshipers of images [*pesel*] are put to shame, those who make their boast in worthless idols ['*elil*]; all gods bow down before him" (Ps 97:7)

- "The idols ['*atsab*] of the nations are silver and gold, the work of human hands" (Ps 135:15).

The prophets consistently rail against the peoples' fascination with idols:

- "Their land is filled with idols ['*elil*]; they bow down to the work of their hands, to what their own fingers have made" (Isa 2:8)

- "So I went in and looked; there, portrayed on the wall all around, were all kinds of creeping things, and loathsome animals, and all the idols [*gillul*] of the house of Israel" (Ezek 8:10).

Sometimes the prophets use sarcastic humor to shame idol worshipers. A written text can hardly do justice to the parody of idol worship in Isaiah 44:

The ironsmith fashions it and works it over the coals, shaping it with hammers, and forging it with his strong arm; he becomes hungry and his strength fails, he drinks no water and is faint. The carpenter stretches a line, marks it out with a stylus, fashions it with planes, and marks it with a compass; he makes it in human form, with human beauty, to be set up in a shrine. He cuts down cedars or chooses a holm tree or an oak and lets it grow strong among the trees of the forest. He plants a cedar and the rain nourishes it. Then it can be used as fuel. Part of it he takes and warms himself; he kindles a fire and bakes bread. Then he makes a god and worships it, makes it a carved image [*pesel*] and bows down before it. Half of it he burns in the fire; over this half he roasts meat, eats it and is satisfied. He also warms himself and says, "Ah, I am warm, I can feel the fire!" The rest of it he makes into a god, his idol [*pesel*], bows down to it and worships it; he prays to it and says, "Save me, for you are my god!" (Isa 44:12–17)

Jeremiah and Hosea likewise use humorous images to effect shame among the people:

For the customs of the peoples are false: a tree from the forest is cut down, and worked with an ax by the hands of an artisan; people deck it with silver and gold; they fasten it with hammer and nails so that it cannot move. Their idols [Hebrew: "they"] are like scarecrows in a cucumber field, and they cannot speak; they have to be carried, for they cannot walk. Do not be afraid of them, for they cannot do evil, nor is it in them to do good. (Jer 10:3–5)

> And now they keep on sinning and make a cast
> image [*massekah*] for themselves, idols [*'atsab*] of
> silver made according to their understanding, all
> of them the work of artisans. "Sacrifice to these,"
> they say. People are kissing calves! (Hos 13:2).

Readers cannot help thinking, "How ridiculous!" By describing the local religious practices in caricature, the prophets encourage the monotheistic, aniconic Israelites to act conversely and even to feel a sense of superiority over the locals. Sadly, caricature of the other's religious practices is still used today as a technique to encourage compliance with a competing orthodoxy.

RITUALS OF THE CULT

We turn now to the worship practices of the cult, perhaps the area most misunderstood by modern readers, who are often offended by the dual excesses of minutia and blood. But we must remember that the theological context for all rituals of the ancient cult is grounded in the faith conviction that what happens in the cult matters to God. Because ritual matters to God, God has commanded the rituals. Consequently, accuracy in minute details is critical. Detailed rituals invoke the divine presence, which is accompanied by divine blessing, the results of which are prosperity, fertility, and long life.

The main source for information about ancient Israelite cultic rituals is the book of Leviticus. As noted above, despite its name, the book primarily addresses worship rituals to be conducted by the Aaronide priests on behalf of the community. The book is the literary center of the Pentateuch, introduced by the book of beginnings (Genesis) and the book of redemption (Exodus) and followed by the book of wilderness wanderings (Numbers) and the book of recapitulation and exhortation (Deuteronomy). The geographical setting for Leviticus is Mt. Sinai, enfolding the matter of cultic ritual into the divine commandments issued to Moses for the benefit of all. These two textual realities (its place at the center of the Pentateuch and its geographic setting at Mt. Sinai) combine to elevate the ritual concerns of Leviticus in the minds and hearts of the ancient audience. Again, we remind readers of the complex editorial history of the Pentateuch. Scholars agree on the Priestly source as the author of Leviticus (who else would care this much about worship ritual?) and on an exilic or postexilic date for its composition. That is, even though the rituals are set in the context of the wilderness, the writing almost certainly represents rituals in effect centuries later and projected back in literary time to their "origin" at Mount Sinai.

A common modern misconception is that the worship rituals of ancient Israel are more or less just an older and more primitive version of a contemporary worship service. Modern readers imagine a congregation gathering on a regular basis and engaging in corporate rituals led by the priest. But worship rituals in ancient Israel were much more solitary than our worship services today. Ancient Israelites primarily went to the temple for specific ritualistic reasons: to offer thanksgiving for a particular blessing, to seek pardon for a particular sin, to seek divine guidance for a particular question. There may have been multiple worshipers at the temple, but each was there with a particular, individual purpose. Except for the three annual festivals at which attendance was mandatory, no regularized services were held at the temple; the weekly gatherings on the Sabbath in synagogues are a much later development.

Purification

The first concern of priests always has to be the purity of the people, places, and things involved in worship. The basic faith conviction behind the concern for purity is simple: God is holy and everything else is not. Before the divine presence is invoked, therefore, people, places, and things must be made holy (obviously, the alternative of making God unholy is not an option). "Holy" (Hebrew: *qodesh*) in biblical texts means "set apart" for something sacred. Although the word has taken on moral connotations in modern parlance, in biblical use the word does not carry the weight of moral judgment. To be holy is to be set apart or distinct or separated for divine contact. At this point, astute readers will remember the priestly language of Genesis 1, in which God separates the elements of creation. As we noted in connection with language of separation, the function of priests can be described as separating things into their rightful categories. The most succinct job description for priests appears in Lev 10:10: "You are to distinguish [lit. "cause to separate"] between the holy [*qodesh*] and the common, and between the unclean and the clean."

People, places, time, and objects naturally and regularly existed in states described as common or clean. Actions or processes, whether human-initiated or nature-initiated, moved common and clean things into the categories of holy or unclean. Most modern readers can grasp the concept of a particular ritual that moves an item from common to holy, since most of us have witnessed such rituals of dedication, consecration, or ordination. Harder for the modern mindset is the ancient notion of clean and unclean, probably because of the modern association of the word *unclean* with the notion that something is morally unsatisfactory. In the ancient world, the category of the unclean is not a moral category; it is a ritual category in that items that are unclean are not eligible to be in contact with the divine realm. But, to repeat, items naturally occurred as clean; something moved an object from clean to unclean and back again. The ancient mindset may be depicted below:

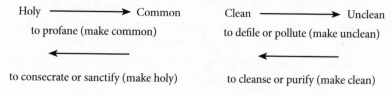

Holy ⟶ Common
to profane (make common)
⟵
to consecrate or sanctify (make holy)

Clean ⟶ Unclean
to defile or pollute (make unclean)
⟵
to cleanse or purify (make clean)

Some examples may help. Bodily fluids naturally occur in a state inside the body: seminal fluid is inside the genitals; the womb lining is inside the uterus; white blood cells are inside the body. When semen or menstrual blood or skin eruptions occur, they occur outside their normal state and are thus "unclean." In other words, the bodily fluids normally occurring inside the body break the natural boundaries and manifest themselves outside the body. The fact that these eruptive processes are "natural" is irrelevant to the logic. The key is that the object is not in its "rightful place." Again, modern readers should not equate the biblical category of unclean with the contemporary pejorative "dirty." Seminal emissions and menstrual bleeding are natural processes necessary for procreation, yet they render a person unclean. Furthermore, the objects rendered unclean include not only the person but other objects contaminated by the uncleanness. Leviticus 15 specifies that seminal emissions render the bed or anything the man sits on or touches to be unclean. Not only that, but any person who sits on what the man sat on becomes unclean, and so on. The image of contagion or infection comes to mind as an apt metaphor for uncleanness in the Bible. Once the object has moved from clean to unclean, a purification ritual is needed to restore it to the category of clean. Purification rituals usually involve separating oneself from the rest of the community, bathing, washing objects, and sacrificial offerings.

There are unclean objects specified in the biblical texts with no prescribed ritual for purifying them so as to make them clean. Specifically, we refer to the unclean animals listed in Leviticus 11. We can begin to understand the distinction between clean and unclean animals by paying attention to the ancient mindset of "how things ought to be." So, for example, creatures that live in the waters "ought" to have fins and scales; those are clean (Lev 11:9). Sea creatures without fins and scales are unclean because they are not fulfilling the mandates of their intended category. Four-footed animals "ought" to be cleft-footed and chew the cud; those are clean (Lev 11:3). Animals otherwise constructed are unclean, including the camel, the rock badger, the hare, and the pig. Winged insects "ought" to fly; those are clean. Winged insects that walk on all fours are unclean (Lev 11:20). Exception is made for winged insects with jointed legs, because apparently they leap rather than walk, strictly speaking (Lev 11:21). The distinction of clean and unclean animals was vital in keeping the various dietary laws. In later Hebrew and Aramaic, this proper distinction would be known as *kashrut* (literally, "proper") from which the word *kosher* derives.

A clean object is eligible to be consecrated or sanctified so that it moves into a state of holiness. At no time may an unclean object come into contact with a holy object. The resulting contamination for the community would be unbearable, because divine contact of any kind would no longer be possible. Great care, therefore, is taken to attend to purification and consecration rituals for any people or objects connected with the sanctuary, whether to the tabernacle or to the temple. All the furniture, vestments, utensils, and people are purified and consecrated for sacred use. The minutia of the biblical texts, though mind-numbing to modern readers, guarantees the proper rituals will be performed to invoke the divine presence and divine blessing.

Sacrificial Offerings

Ritual offerings to the deity were common to all the cultures of the ancient Near East. Animals, agricultural produce, and sons were the primary measures of prosperity in the ancient world. To transfer wealth from human ownership to the divine realm was indeed a sacrifice, in the sense of surrendering something of worth for the sake of something more valuable. In the world of the cult, the "something more valuable" was the divine presence. Despite the plethora of details in Leviticus related to the rituals themselves, biblical texts nowhere fully explain what we would call today the theological doctrine of sacrifice. In many ways, sacrifice is simply assumed by the biblical texts as the way of being in relationship with God. That is, the relationship between God and the people of God is the basis for making sense of sacrifice, rather than the reverse. Sacrifice does not create the relationship; rather, sacrifice maintains or strengthens the already-existing relationship. When humans perceive the relationship as torn or broken, sacrifice serves as evidence of the human desire to repair and restore it. There is rarely the sense of appeasement of an angry deity through sacrifice in the biblical texts; rather, sacrifice serves as concrete evidence of human acknowledgement of the ruptured relationship and of the desire for restoration. In theological-speak, restoration of the divine-human relationship is *atonement*, sometimes helpfully spelled "at-one-ment" to highlight the purpose of bringing the relationship back into equilibrium.

The most important offerings involve animal sacrifice as the means of atonement, because of the importance of blood. Blood in the ancient world was already known to be the essential ingredient for life. Observation alone reveals that when human or animal loses its blood, it dies. Reason, therefore, announces that blood is life. In the words of Gen 9:4, "Only, you shall not eat flesh with its life, that is, its blood." Or in Lev 17:14, "For the life of every creature—its blood is its life; therefore I have said to the people of Israel: You shall not eat the blood of any creature, for the life of every creature is its blood; whoever eats it shall be cut off." In the primordial story of Cain and Abel, God confronts Cain because "your brother's blood is crying out to me from the ground" (Gen 4:10). Abel's blood, now anthropomorphized, represents Abel's life-force that survives his earthly existence and is capable of crying out to God for redress. Because blood was understood to have this power inherent in it, blood was the perfect agent for purification and consecration rituals. It served, to use a somewhat crude image, as a divine detergent, washing away sin and impurity of any kind. We may think of the seemingly oxymoronic phrase from Christian spirituals, "washed in the blood of the Lamb." Here as well, blood is the purifying agent that cleanses completely.

Turning to the rituals of animal sacrifice, we note two different types of sacrificial rituals, distinguished by the end use of the animal. Both types take place at the altar erected in the open outer courtyard of the temple, and both are carried out by priests. As noted above, the Hebrew word for "altar," *mizbeach*, comes from the verb *z-b-ch* ("slaughter") and means literally "place of slaughter." The Greek word for altar, *thysiasterion*, means literally "sacrifice-station." In one type of ritual, the whole animal is burned upon the altar. The Hebrew word for this type of sacrifice is *'olah*, translated as "burnt offering" or "whole burnt offering." (Transliteration of the Hebrew word *'olah* into Greek and then into German led to the word "holocaust.") The first chapter of Leviticus specifies the rituals surrounding this type of sacrifice. The animal must be "a male without blemish" (Lev 1:3, 10), slaughtered at the altar by the priest. The blood is then drained out of the animal and dashed against all sides of the altar (Lev 1:5, 11, 14). After cutting the animal into pieces, the priest arranges the pieces on the altar. "Then the priest shall turn the whole into smoke on the altar as a burnt offering [*'olah*], an offering by fire of pleasing odor to the LORD" (Lev 1:9; also 1:13, 17). The main point seems to be that the animal is offered by the worshiper for no earthly purpose other than because God enjoys it. The sacrifice is an offering of praise. The language may be primitive (a "pleasing odor to the LORD"), but the sacrifice is real and valuable. The biblical texts generally assume that the sacrificial animal will be from the "herd" (that is, cattle or oxen) or from the "flock" (that is, sheep or goats). But provisions are also made for those worshipers who are not wealthy enough to own herds or flocks. In that case, turtledoves or pigeons are acceptable sacrificial offerings (Lev 1:14–17).

In the other type of ritual, the sacrificial animal is only partly burned on the altar, and the remaining portion is distributed as food for priest or worshiper. The Hebrew word for this type of sacrifice is *zebach*, again from the verb *z-b-ch* ("slaughter"). The *zebach* sacrifice may be either male or female from the herd or from the flock. Until the time of burning, the ritual is the same as the *'olah*: the priest slaughters the animal at the altar, drains the blood, and dashes it against all sides of the altar. With the animal ready for burning, the ritual diverges from the *'olah*. The priest removes from the animal "the fat that covers the entrails and all the fat that is around the entrails; the two kidneys with the fat that is on them at the loins, and the appendage of the liver, which he shall remove with the kidneys" (Lev 3:3–4). "Then the priest shall turn these into smoke on the altar as a food offering by fire for a pleasing odor. All fat is the LORD's. It shall be a perpetual statute throughout your generations, in all your settlements: you must not eat any fat or any blood" (Lev 3:16–17). In other words, the fatty parts of the animal are burned on the altar as "food" for the deity, but the rest of the animal is available as food for humans. Supporting priests through offerings was the regular practice throughout the ancient Near East. Their full-time occupation as cultic ritualists did not afford them an opportunity to gain necessary provisions on their own. But cynical readers will recognize the possibility for corruption at this point. Since the priests have the power to legislate sacrificial rituals, greed and the desire for self-gratification could lead to regulations that benefit the priestly appetite at the expense of the peasant worshiper. And in fact, biblical texts note this development; the most offensive example is by Eli's sons.

> Now the sons of Eli were scoundrels; they had no regard for the LORD or for the duties of the priests to the people. When anyone offered sacrifice, the priest's servant would come, while the meat was boiling, with a three-pronged fork in his hand, and he would thrust it into the pan, or kettle, or caldron, or pot; all that the fork brought up the priest would take for himself. This is what they did at Shiloh to all the Israelites who came there. Moreover, before the fat was burned, the priest's servant would come and say to the one who was sacrificing, "Give meat for the priest to roast; for he will not accept boiled meat from you, but only raw." And if the man said to him, "Let them burn the fat first, and then take whatever you wish," he would say, "No, you must give it now; if not, I will take it by force." Thus the sin of the young men was very great in the sight of the LORD; for they treated the offerings of the LORD with contempt. (1 Sam 2:12–17)

Bel and the Dragon, an apocryphal writing from the second century BCE, describes greedy priests in Babylon who "made a hidden entrance [into the cult-statue room], through which they used to go in regularly and consume the provisions" (Bel 13). Even Josephus, writing in the mid-first century CE, notes the propensity for the higher-level priests to take more than their fair share, with the result that the lower-level priests almost starve to death.

In its pristine design, animal sacrifice serves to maintain or restore the relationship between deity and humans. The best animals are offered as a symbol of humanity's best intentions. The blood, symbol of life itself, is used to sanctify the altar of sacrifice. The smoke given up by burning the animal in whole or in part rises to the deity's abode in heaven as a "pleasing odor." The human worshiper has given up something of great value and, in return, has received some things of even greater value: relationship with God, the assurance of the divine presence, and divine blessing.

Besides animals, Leviticus describes other sacrificial offerings of agricultural produce that serve to maintain or restore the divine-human relationship. According to Leviticus 2, grain offerings of the choicest flour should be mixed with (olive) oil and frankincense, a handful of which is then burned on the altar, "an offering by fire of pleasing odor to the LORD" (Lev 2:2, 9, 16). The first fruits of the harvest are to be offered to God on the day after the concluding Sabbath of the festival of unleavened bread (Lev 23:9–14).

The tithe is the regularized offering of one-tenth of produce to the deity, commonly practiced throughout the ancient Near East. Related to the Hebrew word for "ten" (*'eśer*), the tithe in Israel was called the *maśer* and was to be brought to the temple: "But you shall seek the place that the LORD your God will choose out of all your tribes as his habitation to put his name there. You shall go there, bringing there your burnt offerings (*'olah*) and your sacrifices (*zebach*), your tithes (*maśer*) and your donations, your votive gifts, your freewill offerings, and the firstlings of your herds and flocks" (Deut 12:5–6). We can see from this list that offerings to the temple were not restricted to sacrificial animals and tithes. One item expressly prohibited is the sacrifice of children. Though neighboring cultures practiced child sacrifice, Israel's priestly regulations forbade it, even though the principle of the firstborn's belonging to God still held sway. "All that first opens the womb is mine, all your male livestock, the firstborn of cow and sheep. The firstborn of a donkey you shall redeem with a lamb, or if you will not redeem it you shall break its neck. All the firstborn of your sons you shall redeem. No one shall appear before me empty-handed" (Exod 34:19–20). Redemption of the firstborn sons is understood to be accomplished by the dedication of Levites to priestly service. "I hereby accept the Levites from among the Israelites as substitutes for all the firstborn that open the womb among the Israelites. The Levites shall be mine, for all the firstborn are mine; when I killed all the firstborn in the land of Egypt, I consecrated for my own all the firstborn in Israel, both human and animal; they shall be mine. I am the LORD" (Num 3:12–13).

Other Rituals

Priests were set apart for full-time service of God, meticulously following sacrificial rituals to maintain or restore the divine-human relationship. Their constant invocation of the divine presence through sacrificial rituals naturally meant that people would come to them for intercessory prayer and divine guidance. Examples of intercessory prayer abound in biblical texts, a phenomena still practiced today and quite understandable to modern readers. Somewhat less understandable are the methods used to gauge the divine will. We know from temple archives in the ancient Near East that determining and interpreting the will of the gods was big business. Texts from Mesopotamia mention incantation specialists, diviners, omen experts, astronomers, astrologers, cult prophets, exorcists, conjurers, and magicians. The primary means of accessing the divine realm were reading the stars or reading animal entrails. Patterns detected in the heavens or in the innards were then interpreted to the petitioner, who was moved by gratitude to present an offering. The orthodox authors of Deuteronomy expressly prohibit such practices: "No one shall be found among you who makes a son or daughter pass through fire, or who practices divination, or is a soothsayer, or an augur, or a sorcerer, or one who casts spells, or who consults ghosts or spirits, or who seeks oracles from the dead" (Deut 18:10–11). Instead, the ancient Israelites depended primarily on direct communication with God through conversation or dreams. Otherwise, priests could use something like dice called Urim and Thummin to determine the divine will. We see such an example in an episode involving King Saul, his son Jonathan, and the army. King Saul inquired of God's will regarding fighting the Philistines, but received no answer. "Then Saul said, 'O LORD God of Israel, why have you not answered your servant today? If this guilt is in me or in my son Jonathan, O LORD God of Israel, give Urim; but if this guilt is in your people Israel, give Thummim.'

And Jonathan and Saul were indicated by the lot, but the people were cleared. Then Saul said, 'Cast the lot between me and my son Jonathan.' And Jonathan was taken" (1 Sam 14:41–42). Unbeknownst to Saul, Jonathan had disobeyed his orders to fast in preparation for battle.

Cultic Calendar

As noted at the beginning of the chapter, ancient Israelite worship was seldom a communal activity. Most of the time, sacrifices were offered by individuals in gratitude for some particular event (birth, healing, good crop, etc.) or as a purification ritual. Probably reflecting later developments in Israel, the Old Testament instructs the whole community of Israel to assemble for three major festivals. Cultic calendars are found in Exod 23:10–19 and 34:18–26; Lev 23:1–44; and Deut 16:1–17. In short, "Three times a year all your males shall appear before the LORD your God at the place that he will choose: at the festival of unleavened bread, at the festival of weeks, and at the festival of booths. They shall not appear before the LORD empty-handed; all shall give as they are able, according to the blessing of the LORD your God that he has given you" (Deut 16:16–17). In each of the cultic calendars, appearing in assembly is linked with presenting offerings (back) to God. First, the people of Israel are commanded to celebrate the festival of unleavened bread in the first month of the year, from the fourteenth to the twenty-first. In the calendar adopted from the Babylonians, the new year began in the spring, consistent with the new life evident in the herds, flocks, and crops. The festival probably originated as a celebration among agriculturalists in thanksgiving for the blessings of new growth. In Israelite lore, the festival became linked to the exodus from Egypt, in which the people are instructed to be ready to leave with little or no notice, and thus without time to leaven the bread. The Passover festival may have originated among nomadic herdsmen using sacrifice of the first-born as a way to ward off evil and guarantee strength and virility of the flocks and herds. Connected in the biblical texts with the slaying of the first-born of Egypt, the Passover festival coupled with the festival of unleavened bread serves as one extended celebration of God's liberating event. We see the combination in the most developed cultic calendar in Leviticus: "In the first month, on the fourteenth day of the month, at twilight, there shall be a Passover offering to the LORD, and on the fifteenth day of the same month is the festival of unleavened bread to the LORD; seven days you shall eat unleavened bread" (Lev 23:5-6).

The second mandatory festival for the whole community was the Festival of Weeks or First Fruits. Intended to celebrate the spring wheat harvest, the cultic calendar specifies a period of seven Sabbaths between the festival of unleavened bread and the festival of weeks/first fruits. The Greek name for the festival, Pentecost, notes the passage of fifty (*pente*) days. At this festival, the assembly offers new grain, loaves of bread, and lambs as first fruits to God. Later developments linked this festival with the giving of the Torah at Mt. Sinai.

The third mandatory festival was in the fall to celebrate the ingathering of the autumn harvest of fruits and grapes. Based on the Babylonian calendar that fixes the new year in the spring, the Festival of Ingathering is prescribed for the seventh month (Lev 23:39). But the biblical texts betray an older Israelite calendar that fixes the new year in the autumn: "You shall observe the festival of in-gathering *at the end of the year*, when you gather in from the field the fruit of your labor" (Exod 23:16b, author's emphasis; see also Exod 34:22). Perhaps inherited from Canaanite neighbors, this calendar begins the new year (Hebrew *rosh hashanah*) with the Day of Atonement (*yom kippur*) followed by the Festival of Ingathering or Booths. The cultic calendar in Leviticus calls for the community to construct temporary dwellings from branches and leaves: "You shall live in booths for seven days; all that are citizens in Israel shall live in booths, so that your generations may know that I made the people of Israel live in booths when I brought them out of the land of Egypt: I am the LORD your God" (Lev 23:42–43). No matter their ancient origins, the three communal festivals remind Israel of God's redemptive work in the past and give thanks for God's continued blessings in the present.

UNORTHODOX WORSHIP PRACTICES

Until this point, we have described what may be called the "orthodox" cult, since we have used the laws and narratives written by the orthodox priests and preserved in the Old Testament canon. Now we turn to the other side, as it were, reading between the lines of orthodox texts and reading directly the lines of other texts to ferret out what some have called "popular" or "folk" religion, by which is usually meant the worship practices of the majority of regular folk.

The first strategy is to read the opposite side, so to speak, of the orthodox texts we have already considered.

We noted the choice of Jerusalem/Mt. Zion as "the place that the LORD your God will choose out of all your tribes as his habitation to put his name there" (Deut 12:5). Deuteronomic emphasis on one central location for the cult implies that multiple sites were in popular use. The characteristics of the Israelite cult—exclusive and aniconic—receive repeated attention in the biblical texts, probably because people were fascinated with other local deities who were represented by images. Similarly, the explicit prohibition of divination and sorcery surely implicates the Israelites as engaging in such practices. Why else would there be any need to forbid these things? We can cite biblical texts that address these very issues.

Recall the strange story of Saul and the witch of Endor in 1 Samuel 28. The Philistines are once again threatening Israel, so Saul seeks to ascertain the divine will. "When Saul inquired of the LORD, the LORD did not answer him, not by dreams, or by Urim, or by prophets" (1 Sam 28:6). Desperate for guidance, Saul consults a female medium, asking her to bring up Samuel from the dead. She demurs at first but then complies with his request. Samuel appears and complains, "Why have you disturbed me by bringing me up?" (1 Sam 28:15). Saul explains the situation, begging for advice on what to do, at which point Samuel announces his impending defeat at the hands of the Philistine army. Even though orthodox texts explicitly denounce mediums and necromancy, this text presents the incident with realistic dialogue and predictable outcomes. Later, God warns the prophet Isaiah what will happen when people demand that prophets consult the dead: "Now if people say to you, 'Consult the ghosts and the familiar spirits that chirp and mutter; should not a people consult their gods, the dead on behalf of the living, for teaching and for instruction?' Surely, those who speak like this will have no dawn!" (Isa 8:19–20). In the background of these texts is the widespread practice of ancestor worship in the ancient Near East, the belief that the dead could and would communicate with the living to offer guidance and support. In Mesopotamian texts, *kispu* is the Assyrian term used for the regular offerings of food and drink to deceased ancestors. Through the invocation of the names of the deceased ancestors, current familial identity is linked to the past. By honoring the dead with religious rites including food and drink, the living descendants hoped to enjoy beneficence and prosperity.

We turn now to the issue of cultic figurines in ancient Israel. Perhaps the best known story related to figurines is the narrative in Genesis 31, when Jacob, Rachel, and Leah decide to secretly flee from Laban after twenty years of service. The episode begins, "Now Laban had gone to shear his sheep, and Rachel stole her father's household gods" (Gen 31:19). When Laban realizes they have left, he pursues them and accuses Jacob, "Even though you had to go because you longed greatly for your father's house, why did you steal my gods?" (Gen 31:30). Jacob, of course, denies any knowledge of theft and promises to kill anyone found with the stolen property. Tension mounts as Laban searches the tents of Jacob, Leah, and the two maids. Finally, he enters Rachel's tent. "Now Rachel had taken the household gods and put them in the camel's saddle, and sat on them. Laban felt all about in the tent, but did not find them. And she said to her father, 'Let not my lord be angry that I cannot rise before you, for the way of women is upon me.' So he searched, but did not find the household gods" (Gen 31:34–35).

Household gods, Hebrew *teraphim*, also play a part in the narrative about the migration of the tribe of Dan in Judges 17–18. The basic plot outline is that a man living in the hill country north of Jerusalem made a household shrine and stocked it with a cast idol (*massekah*), a priestly vestment known as the ephod, and *teraphim*. When the Danites were migrating from the southeastern coast to an area northwest of the Sea of Galilee, they stopped at the shrine and looted the cast idol, the ephod, and the teraphim. When the shrine's priest objected, the six hundred armed Danites replied, "Keep quiet! Put your hand over your mouth, and come with us, and be to us a father and a priest. Is it better for you to be priest to the house of one person, or to be priest to a tribe and clan in Israel? Then the priest accepted the offer. He took the ephod, the teraphim, and the idol, and went along with the people" (Judg 18:19–20).

One other strange incident: when David needed to escape the murderous rage of Saul, David's wife Michal helped him escape. Then "Michal took an idol [*teraphim*] and laid it on the bed; she put a net of goats' hair on its head, and covered it with the clothes" (1 Sam 19:13). From these texts, we learn that *teraphim* were small enough to hide under a camel's saddle and woman's skirt and are transportable, yet large enough to imitate a sleeping man. They were designed for shrines in homes, but may have also accompanied nomads. Excavations in Syria-Palestine have unearthed thousands of small figurines. Many have exaggerated reproductive features, probably to give emphasis to the god's or goddess's ability to bring about fertility and prosperity.

Other texts indicate that deities were represented at public shrines with larger symbols. The predominant deities of Canaan were Ba'al, the storm god, and his consort Asherah. From what we can tell from textual and artifact evidence, Ba'al was represented at shrines by pillars, probably calling to mind the male phallus and emphasizing Ba'al's pivotal role in providing life-sustaining rain. Asherah was represented by wooden poles, either live trees or carved posts in the shape of the female vulva, suggesting the life-giving role of the female deity. Outdoor shrines to Ba'al and/or Asherah were constructed on hills, consistent with the ancient Near Eastern belief that mountains were sacred spaces for gods. The biblical criticism of Israelite worship of deities other than the God of Israel at places other than Jerusalem is pervasive. For example, "For they also built for themselves high places, pillars, and sacred poles [*asherah*] on every high hill and under every green tree; there were also male temple prostitutes in the land. They committed all the abominations of the nations that the LORD drove out before the people of Israel" (1 Kgs 14:23–24); "The people of Israel secretly did things that were not right against the LORD their God. They built for themselves high places at all their towns, from watchtower to fortified city; they set up for themselves pillars and sacred poles [*asherah*] on every high hill and under every green tree; there they made offerings on all the high places, as the nations did whom the LORD carried away before them. They did wicked things, provoking the LORD to anger" (2 Kgs 17:9–11). The reference to temple prostitutes may refer to cultic activities that took place at the shrines in an attempt to induce the gods to bring about fertility. Jacob's son Judah inquires about "the temple prostitute who was at Enaim by the wayside," to whom he needs to make good his pledge of a goat (Gen 38:21). The Hebrew word translated as "temple prostitute" is *qadeshah*, intimately related to the root *q-d-sh*, "to be holy." Orthodox Deuteronomy feels the need to prohibit such behavior: "None of the daughters of Israel shall be a temple prostitute [*qadeshah*]; none of the sons of Israel shall be a temple prostitute [*qadesh*]" (Deut 23:17). King Asa of Judah is praised by the authors of 1 Kings because "He put away the male temple prostitutes [*qadesh*] out of the land, and removed all the idols [*gillul*] that his ancestors had made. He also removed his mother Maacah from being queen mother, because she had made an abominable image for Asherah; Asa cut down her image and burned it at the Wadi Kidron"(1 Kgs 15:12–13). The appetite for temple prostitutes must have been substantial, since Asa's son Jehoshaphat dealt with the same issue. "The remnant of the male temple prostitutes [*qadesh*] who were still in the land in the days of his father Asa, he exterminated" (1 Kgs 22:46). More than two centuries later, King Josiah faced a worse problem: the temple prostitutes and devotees of Asherah were resident in the Jerusalem Temple. "He broke down the houses of the male temple prostitutes [*qadesh*] that were in the house of the LORD, where the women did weaving for Asherah" (2 Kgs 23:7). Scholars are currently debating the significance of an inscription excavated from a caravan way-station in the Negeb desert in southern Israel reading, "YHWH and his A/asherah." The controversy is over whether the last word should be capitalized or not; Asherah would be a direct reference to the goddess, the consort of Ba'al, whereas asherah would be a reference to the symbolic vulvic-shaped pole. So the inscription clearly associates the God of Israel with either a Canaanite goddess or with an image; either is an abomination to the orthodox cult.

The prophets, as we noted in chapter two, railed against the people's forsaking the God of the covenant. "For the teraphim utter nonsense, and the diviners see lies; the dreamers tell false dreams, and give empty consolation. Therefore the people wander like sheep; they suffer for lack of a shepherd" (Zech 10:2). The most comprehensive rebuke comes from the prophet we call Third Isaiah, who criticizes child sacrifice, fornication, worship of false gods, incubation rituals, and divining:

> Whom are you mocking? Against whom do you open your mouth wide and stick out your tongue? Are you not children of transgression, the offspring of deceit—you that burn with lust among the oaks, under every green tree; you that slaughter your children in the valleys, under the clefts of the rocks? Among the smooth stones of the valley is your portion; they, they, are your lot; to them you have poured out a drink offering, you have brought a grain offering. Shall I be appeased for these things? Upon a high and lofty mountain you have set your bed, and there you went up to offer sacrifice. Behind the door and the doorpost you have set up your symbol; for, in deserting me, you have uncovered your bed, you have gone up to it, you have made it wide; and you have made a bargain for yourself with them, you have loved their bed, you have gazed on their nakedness. You journeyed to Molech [chief god of the Ammonites] with oil, and multiplied your

perfumes; you sent your envoys far away, and
sent down even to Sheol [the place of the dead].
(Isa 57:4–9)

At this point, modern readers are often appalled by
the "pagan" nature of ancient Israelite folk religion, but the
sacrificial rituals of the orthodox cult are unattractive as
well. Lest we judge our ancient ancestors in the faith too
harshly, we should note that all these rituals—orthodox
and unorthodox—grow out of the people's insatiable
hunger for an intimate relationship with God. Sometimes
the relationship with God is nurtured by partaking in the
"orthodox" rituals presided over by Aaronite priests at the
Jerusalem Temple. Sometimes the relationship is nurtured
by all manner of other "unorthodox" rituals in homes and
at local shrines. Remember that the average worshiper
only went to the Jerusalem Temple on the three mandatory festivals and on special occasions. The prevalence of
"unorthodox" worship in ancient Israel gives us a glimpse
into the importance of God to ordinary people in everyday life. Access to the divine will was so integrally related
to their lives that they engaged in many and various ways
to deepen the relationship with God. Remember, assess-
ment of rituals as orthodox or not is the prerogative of the
priests. Apparently, such pronouncements from on high,
so to speak, drove a large segment of the population "underground," where they could engage in relationship with
God through other means. One conclusion could be that
the religious leaders were out of touch with the real needs
of the people, a sober warning for any religious leaders
today. The Old Testament witnesses to a deep longing to
know the LORD, whether by "orthodox" or "unorthodox"

means. As St. Augustine, Bishop of North Africa, eloquent-
ly prayed near the end of the fourth century CE, "You have
made us for yourself, O Lord, and our hearts are restless
until they rest in you."

FOUR

Character

CHARACTER IS DIFFICULT TO define, but as with great art or base pornography, we know it when we see it. We may call someone a *character*, by which we usually mean that the person is eccentric or out of the mainstream. Or we may admire someone who has *character*, by which we usually mean a sense of right and wrong, or ethics. This chapter explores the second sense of the word. Moral character is an important theme in the Old Testament; this is attested by the many texts that encourage or prescribe certain behaviors and by the numerous texts that denounce other behaviors. If we have convinced readers by now that the themes explored in the previous chapters are crucial to understanding the Old Testament, then we may fruitfully return to those themes to consider how character is formed so that virtue prevails. We conclude with a brief discussion of the character of God.

CREATION: GOODNESS

Recall the opening chapter of Genesis. God orders the cosmos with structure and content, pronouncing it "good" and "very good" a total of seven times. Used almost 750 times, some form of the Hebrew word *tob*, "good," is found in every book of the Old Testament except Obadiah,

Habakkuk, and Haggai. English translations will use of variety of words in translation, due to the breadth of meaning of the Hebrew *tob*: the meaning ranges from a utilitarian description to a philosophical category. Our concern is with goodness in its role in formation of human character, especially as it relates to creation. In that regard, therefore, the sevenfold repetition of *tob* in Genesis 1 illumines our reading of the Creator's intent. Creation is good because the various elements fulfill the purpose for which they were created. To take one example, God made the sun and moon to rule over the day and night and to give light on the earth. Inasmuch as they do so, they are good. We noted in chapter 1 the first use of "not good" in the Bible in Gen 2:18, when God realizes that it is "not good" for the *'adam* to be alone. The woman is created as a partner for the man, and insofar as the two creatures live in partnership, life is good. The first chapters of Genesis lead us to the conclusion that goodness is built into the structure of the universe. Goodness is evident when the creation does what God intended it to do: lights give light, swarming creatures swarm, creeping things creep, the earth sprouts vegetation, animals and humans multiply, and Sabbath rest is hallowed. Readers will remember that ritual purity laws take account of this good order of the universe in their categories of clean and unclean.

But, of course, with humans in the creative mix, life is not that simple. Human choice spoils the simple, naïve goodness of the opening chapters of Genesis. Thus, the biblical texts address the moral issue of discerning good (*tob*) and evil (*ra'*), a contrast that occurs over seventy-five times in the Old Testament. Discerning good and evil is the biblical equivalent of distinguishing between right and wrong. Just as they deal with the establishment of goodness in the structure of the cosmos, so the opening chapters of Genesis also address the moral nature of goodness by introducing "the tree of the knowledge of good and evil" in Gen 2:9. Partaking of the fruit of this appealing tree will play out by the end of chapter 3, when the humans' choice rips the fabric of creation.

Other texts testify to the human experience that creation is not working as it should. The righteous Job laments to God, "But when I looked for good [*tob*], evil [*ra'*] came; and when I waited for light, darkness came" (Job 30:26). Job's words would only be an effective complaint if the situation he describes is unnatural and unexpected. The prophet Isaiah denounces the people of Judah with stinging words: "Ah, you who call evil good and good evil, who put darkness for light and light for darkness, who put bitter for sweet and sweet for bitter" (Isa 5:20)! Clearly, the prophet is criticizing the people for turning the nature of the cosmos upside-down. Just a few verses later, he is more specific as to the nature of their evil: they "acquit the guilty for a bribe, and deprive the innocent of their rights! . . . For they have rejected the instruction of the LORD of hosts; and have despised the word of the Holy One of Israel" (Isa 5:23, 24b). A similar complaint is lodged by the prophet Malachi when he accuses the people of wearying God "by saying, 'All who do evil are good in the sight of the LORD, and he delights in them.' Or by asking, 'Where is the God of justice?'" (Mal 2:17). When people fail to discern good and evil, they corrupt creation and offend the Creator. A common prophetic indictment is that the people love evil more than good (see Isa 52:3; Mic 3:2).

As we have said, the underlying assumption is that goodness is woven into the fabric of the universe and is discernible to humans, especially to those humans who are chosen by God to rule as kings. Solomon, the biblical paragon of wisdom, upon his accession to the throne, prays, "Give your servant therefore an understanding mind to govern your people, able to discern between good [*tob*] and evil [*ra'*]; for who can govern this your great people" (1 Kgs 3:9)? In another example, a supplicant to King David fawns, "Your servant thought, 'The word of my lord the king will set me at rest'; for my lord the king is like the angel of God, discerning good and evil. The LORD your God be with you!" (1 Sam 14:17).

The Old Testament's notion of goodness includes the ability not only to distinguish it from evil but to *choose* goodness over evil when presented with the choice. Amos, the fierce champion of justice and righteousness, illustrates the point: "Seek good [*tob*] and not evil [*ra'*], that you may live; and so the LORD, the God of hosts, will be with you, just as you have said. Hate evil [*ra'*] and love good [*tob*], and establish justice in the gate; it may be that the LORD, the God of hosts, will be gracious to the remnant of Joseph" (Amos 5:14–15). As we have seen in other passages cited above, we see the connection here between good and justice. The author of Deuteronomy is even more explicit: "See, I have set before you today life and prosperity [*tob*], death and adversity [*ra'*]" (Deut 30:15). The parallelism of the verse demands that we see the contrasts of life and death on the one hand and good and evil on the other hand. Life and good are opposed to death and evil. The plea for moral choice follows in verse 19: "Choose life so that you and your descendants may live." Obviously, choosing life means choosing the good.

For Western readers steeped in the Augustinian notion of moral depravity, the idea that humans can choose the good may seem naïve. But in this regard, the biblical texts exhibit a higher anthropology than the early church fathers, calling for the people of Israel to choose good and reject evil, and holding the underlying assumption that they actually can do so. This potential to choose the good is built into creation and is possible through devotion to the Creator. Because God is good, those who love God are able to choose the good. Assertions of God's goodness are abundant in the Old Testament; they include, "O give thanks to the LORD, for he is good" (Ps 106:1; 107:1; 118:1; 1 Chr 16:34). By trusting in God's goodness, humanity is able to trust that following God's commands will be the equivalent of choosing the good. Two psalms (among many) may be cited in this regard: "Come, O children, listen to me; I will teach you the fear of the LORD. Which of you desires life, and covets many days to enjoy good [*tob*]? Keep your tongue from evil [*ra'*], and your lips from speaking deceit. Depart from evil [*ra'*], and do good [*tob*], seek peace, and pursue it" (Ps 34:11–14); "Trust in the LORD, and do good [*tob*]" (Ps 37:3).

COVENANT: JUSTICE

As was discussed in chapter 2, God's covenant with Israel is the principal metaphor for God's permanent relationship with this people as Sovereign. Human behavior is stipulated by the Sovereign and ratified by the people in their obedience to the Sovereign's stipulations. Obedience to the covenant brings about long life; fertility of land, animals, and humans; and blessings galore. But what character traits are fostered by obedience to the covenant? The primary character trait of the individuals and community who live in obedience to God's covenant is justice for all members of society. God, who enters into covenant, is concerned about justice, and therefore the people should learn to be concerned about justice. We have already noted that the book of Deuteronomy follows the ancient Near Eastern format of a treaty, with the first eleven chapters serving as hortatory prologue to the laws enumerated in chapters 12–26. As Moses comes to the end of his sermonic introduction to the assembly, he summarizes the covenant relationship.

> So now, O Israel, what does the LORD your God require of you? Only to fear the LORD your God, to walk in all his ways, to love him, to serve the LORD your God with all your heart and with all your soul, and to keep the commandments of the LORD your God and his decrees that I am commanding you today, for your own well-being. . . . For the LORD your God is God of gods and Lord of lords, the great God, mighty and awesome, who is not partial and takes no bribe, who executes justice for the orphan and the widow, and who loves the strangers, providing them food and clothing. You shall also love the stranger, for you were strangers in the land of Egypt. (Deut 10:12–13, 17–19)

Of all the things that could be said about the covenant-making God, the primary character trait highlighted here is concern for justice. The most common Hebrew word for justice is *mishpat*, from the Hebrew root *sh-p-t*. At its core, to *sh-p-t* means to govern in such a way that equitable rights are established for the community and for the individuals within the community. The result of this way of life together is *mishpat*. Thus, the Old Testament uses *mishpat* to describe a specific decision made in adjudication ("judgment") as well as the overall cultural atmosphere of communal equity resulting from accumulated individual judgments ("justice"). The one who governs in this way is the *shopet*, rendered in English as "judge" but carrying much broader responsibility that the modern forensic idea of a courtroom judge; we would be better served if the word were translated "governor" or even "legislator." The presence of *mishpat* for individuals and for community is the measure of covenant obedience.

Responsibility for justice resided with the family patriarch during the premonarchial period of Israel's life. As families and clans and tribes came together into confederation, leaders (called "judges" in the Bible) arose at times of crisis to coordinate the communal response to the threat. After the establishment of the monarchy, officials were appointed to deal with adjudicating disputes. The episode recounted in Exodus 18 is probably an attempt to root the practice of local and regional judges in the wilderness experience at Mount Sinai. Careful readers will note that the chapter has virtually no ties to the ones before and after. After some fancy footwork to explain what had been going on with Moses's Midianite family while he was busy liberating his people from Egypt, we hear, "Jethro, Moses's father-in-law, came into the wilderness where Moses was encamped at the mountain of God, bringing Moses' sons and wife to him" (Exod 18:5). But the first verse of the *next* chapter has the Israelites arriving at Mount Sinai "on that very day." At any rate, in small talk over tea the next evening, Jethro criticizes Moses for sitting as judge [*shopet*] all day long: "What is this that you are doing for the people? Why do you sit alone, while all the people stand around you from morning until evening? Moses said to his father-in-law, 'Because the people come to me to inquire of God. When they have a dispute, they come to me and I decide [*shapat*] between one person and another, and I make known to them the statutes and instructions of God'" (Exod 18:14–16). Here we see the connection between the will of God, expressed as the statutes and instructions, and the role of the leader who judges. Concerned about the burden of sitting as judge all day every day, Jethro counsels Moses to appoint some assistant judges.

> You should also look for able men among all the people, men who fear God, are trustworthy, and hate dishonest gain; set such men over them as officers over thousands, hundreds, fifties and tens. Let them sit as judges [*shopet*] for the people at all times; let them bring every important case to you, but decide [*shapat*] every minor case themselves. So it will be easier for you, and they will bear the burden with you. If you do this, and God so commands you, then you will be able to endure, and all these people will go to their home in peace. (Exod 18:21–23)

Legislation in Deuteronomy institutionalizes the system that Jethro advised in the wilderness: "You shall appoint judges [*shopet*] and officials throughout your tribes, in all your towns that the LORD your God is giving you, and they shall render just decisions [*shapat*] for the people" (Deut 16:18). The Chronicler, a late literary source, describes King Jehoshapat (whose name means "YHWH judges") as implementing a similar judicial system: "He appointed judges [*shopet*] in the land in all the fortified cities of Judah, city by city, and said to the judges, 'Consider what you are doing, for you judge [*shapat*] not on behalf of human beings but on the LORD's behalf; he is with you in giving judgment [*shapat*]. Now, let the fear of the LORD be upon you; take care what you do, for there is no perversion of justice [*mishpat*] with the LORD our God, or partiality, or taking of bribes'" (2 Chr 19:5–7).

Rendering justice is clearly associated with acting on God's behalf; humans judge justly because God judges justly. Texts celebrating God as a just judge are especially prevalent in the Psalms. A few examples will suffice: "He judges [*shapat*] the world with righteousness; he judges the peoples with equity" (Ps 9:8; see also 98:9); "Let the nations be glad and sing for joy, for you judge [*shapat*] the peoples with equity and guide the nations upon earth" (Ps 67:4); "for he is coming, for he is coming to judge [*shapat*] the earth. He will judge [*shapat*] the world with righteousness, and the peoples with his truth" (Ps 96:13); "The heavens declare his righteousness, for God himself is judge [*shopet*]" (Ps 50:6). As Sovereign Judge, God stands ready to criticize any who would pervert justice. Psalm 82 depicts God's denouncing the other gods for corrupting *mishpat*: "God has taken his place in the divine council; in the midst of the gods he holds judgment [*shapat*]: 'How long will you judge [*shapat*] unjustly and show partiality to the wicked? Give justice [*mishpat*] to the weak and the orphan; maintain the right of the lowly and the destitute'" (Ps 82:1–3). Those who were denied justice in society clung to the promise that God as Judge would vindicate them: "For he stands at the right hand of the needy, to save them from those who would condemn them to death" (Ps 109:31).

As the chief regent of God on earth, the king had a special responsibility to establish justice. The poetic job description of the king in Psalm 72 calls attention to this: "Give the king your justice [*mishpat*], O God, and your righteousness to a king's son. May he judge [*shapat*] your people with righteousness, and your poor with justice [*mishpat*] . . . May he defend the cause [*shapat*] of the poor of the people, give deliverance to the needy, and crush the oppressor" (Ps 72:1–2, 4). Solomon is praised for his wisdom in rendering justice in the matter of the baby claimed by two women: "All Israel heard of the judgment [*shapat*] that the king had rendered; and they stood in awe of the king, because they perceived that the wisdom of God was in him, to execute justice [*mishpat*]" (1 Kgs 3:28).

Since God establishes justice, those in covenant relationship with God must also establish justice in society. The commandment prohibiting false witness is likely targeted toward assuring justice for those who are charged with wrongdoing. Legislation is also directed toward the judges, who are understandably susceptible to corruption. "You shall not render an unjust judgment [*mishpat*]; you shall not be partial to the poor or defer to the great: with justice [*mishpat*] you shall judge [*shapat*] your neighbor" (Lev 19:15); "You shall not pervert the justice [*mishpat*] due to your poor in their lawsuits" (Exod 23:6). When Moses recounts the wilderness experience, he remembers, "I charged your judges [*shopet*] at that time: 'Give the members of your community a fair hearing, and judge [*shapat*] rightly between one person and another, whether citizen or resident alien. You must not be partial in judging [*shapat*]: hear out the small and the great alike; you shall not be intimidated by anyone, for the judgment [*mishpat*] is God's'" (Deut 1:16–17).

In ancient Israelite society, the gate to the city served as the gathering place for elders, merchants, and townspeople. Excavations of monumental gates from the period of the monarchy reveal chambers or small rooms set near the gate itself. Such areas would have been ideal settings for adjudicating disputes, finalizing legal transactions, bartering for goods, and otherwise carrying on the business of the town. Not unlike today, those with wealth and power were often able to receive a different justice than those with no power or wealth. Those on the margins of society were especially susceptible to mistreatment. For example, the prophets Amos and Zechariah specifically mention the gate as a place of justice: "Hate evil and love good, and establish justice [*mishpat*] in the gate" (Amos 5:15a); "These are the things that you shall do: Speak the truth to one another, render in your gates judgments [*shapat*] that are true and make for peace, do not devise evil in your hearts against one another, and love no false oath; for all these are things that I hate, says the LORD" (Zech 8:16–17). Other prophetic announcements call the community to the covenantal obligation of establishing justice for all, especially the weakest members of society. Biblical "code" for "the weak" is frequently the triad of orphan, widow, and resident alien. Orphans and widows did not have the male relatives (father or husband, respectively) to guarantee their rights in society; the resident alien did not have the ancestral right to property, as did

natural-born Israelites. Each category of individual, therefore, was susceptible to less-than-full participation in the
covenant community. A few prophetic examples suffice to
make the point. "Wash yourselves; make yourselves clean;
remove the evil of your doings from before my eyes; cease
to do evil, learn to do good; seek justice [*mishpat*], rescue
the oppressed, defend the orphan, plead for the widow"
(Isa 1:16–17); "Your princes are rebels and companions of
thieves. Everyone loves a bribe and runs after gifts. They
do not defend [*shapat*] the orphan, and the widow's cause
does not come before them" (Isa 1:23); "Ah, you who make
iniquitous decrees, who write oppressive statutes, to turn
aside the needy from justice [*mishpat*] and to rob the
poor of my people of their right, that widows may be your
spoil, and that you may make the orphans your prey!" (Isa
10:1–2); "They have grown fat and sleek. They know no
limits in deeds of wickedness; they do not judge with justice the cause of the orphan, to make it prosper, and they
do not defend [*shapat*] the rights [*mishpat*] of the needy"
(Jer 5:28); "Thus says the LORD of hosts: Render true
judgments [*mishpat*], show kindness and mercy to one another; do not oppress the widow, the orphan, the alien, or
the poor; and do not devise evil in your hearts against one
another" (Zech 7:9–10). Other prophetic oracles denounce
the general condition of society as a perversion of justice.
For example, "For the vineyard of the LORD of hosts is the
house of Israel, and the people of Judah are his pleasant
planting; he expected justice [*mishpat*], but saw bloodshed
[*mishpach*]; righteousness [*tsedeqah*], but heard a cry
[*tse'aqah*]!" (Isa 5:7; note the word-play in Hebrew where
similar-sounding words have different meanings); "So the
law becomes slack and justice [*mishpat*] never prevails.

The wicked surround the righteous—therefore judgment [*mishpat*] comes forth perverted" (Hab 1:4); "Ah, you that turn justice [*mishpat*] to wormwood, and bring righteousness to the ground" (Amos 5:7)!

That the mark of God's covenantal community is justice is indicated in the great prophetic call of Amos, echoed by prophets ever since: "But let justice [*mishpat*] roll down like waters, and righteousness like an ever-flowing stream" (Amos 5:24). When things are as they should be, kings guarantee everyone's rights, judges judge justly, and people experience justice in community.

CULTUS: HOLINESS

The role of the cultus in ancient Israel was to provide time and space for the indwelling of the divine presence. Rituals of purification were used to set apart people, places, and things as "holy" (*qadosh*), since they would come into contact with the divine holiness of God (see chapter 3, above). Belonging to this holy God in covenant and accessing the divine holiness through the cultus make the people a "treasured possession" out of all the people of the earth (Exod 19:5). The authors of Deuteronomy understand God's particular choice of Israel as a manifestation of Israel's sharing in God's holiness: "For you are a people holy [*qadosh*] to the LORD your God; the LORD your God has chosen you out of all the peoples on earth to be his people, his treasured possession" (Deut 7:6; 14:2). "You shall be holy [*qadosh*] to me; for I the LORD am holy, and I have separated you from the other peoples to be mine" (Lev 20:26). That is, Israel is a people set apart (*qadosh*) from all other peoples, whose vocation in the world is to be a "priestly kingdom and a holy nation" (Exod 19:6).

We made the point in chapter 3 that the Hebrew word *qadosh* does not always carry the moral freight that is in our English word *holy*. (For example, temple furniture can be holy.) But *qadosh* is also a character trait: those who are holy behave in ways that mimic the holy God they worship. After detailed instructions on what creatures may be eaten and not eaten, the summary statement is, "For I am the LORD who brought you up from the land of Egypt, to be your God; you shall be holy, for I am holy" (Lev 11:45). Distinguishing between clean and unclean foods indicates holiness, as does the distinction between pure and impure sexual relations (Leviticus 18). Based on the discussion of the cultus in chapter 3, readers may indeed understand holiness as making a distinction. But the meaning of holiness in the biblical tradition expands to include basic obedience to God's commands: "So you shall remember and do all my commandments, and you shall be holy to your God" (Num 15:40). The nineteenth chapter of Leviticus is a collection of various laws, each of which ends with the motive clause, "I am the LORD." Relevant for our purposes here is the way the chapter begins: "The LORD spoke to Moses saying: Speak to all the congregation of the people of Israel and say to them: You shall be holy, for I the LORD your God am holy" (Lev 19:1–2). All the laws that follow are put in the context of being holy, whether they have any direct connection to the cultus or not. The laws in chapter 19 cover a wide variety of societal situations: revering parents and keeping the Sabbath (vv. 3–4); offering acceptable sacrifices (vv. 5–8); leaving the gleanings of the harvest for the poor (vv. 9–10); not stealing, dealing falsely, lying, or swearing falsely (vv. 11-12); dealing fairly with neighbors and laborers, especially the deaf and the blind (vv. 13–14); rendering justice without partiality (vv. 15–16); not hating kin; and loving the neighbor: "you shall love your neighbor as yourself" (vv. 17–18); keeping proper sexual relations (vv. 19–22); refraining from eating fruit from the orchard until the fifth year (vv. 23–25); not practicing witchcraft, not gashing the flesh, and not getting tattoo marks (vv. 26–28); avoiding both turning daughters into prostitutes and turning to mediums or wizards (vv. 29–31); making sure to "rise before the aged and defer to the old" (v. 32); treating the resident alien with respect (vv. 33–34); and using honest weights and measures (vv. 35–36). According to Leviticus, being holy involves dealing rightly with kin, neighbors, foreigners, land, and animals.

OTHER CHARACTER TRAITS

As we have seen, biblical texts about creation, covenant, and cultus also address proper character for God's people. In addition to these texts, what is called the Wisdom literature also encourages godly character. Texts in this category seek to educate readers in how to succeed in life. To that end, they tend to be filled with practical advice in matters some would classify as "secular," although in the ancient world, the division between secular and sacred is not really applicable. Proverbs, a collection of folk sayings drawn from tradition and human experience, may have been intended to train young boys at the royal court, and therefore they provide excellent clues about the favorable character traits being encouraged. As the first verses of the book tell us, the proverbs are intended "for gaining instruction in wise dealing, righteousness, justice, and equity" (Prov 1:3). Put more enigmatically, "The beginning of wisdom is this: Get wisdom, and whatever else you get, get insight" (Prov 4:7). Wisdom, the summative category for how to succeed in life, is to be taught, sought after, and followed in order to gain the blessings of long life and prosperity.

Those who espouse what has been called the Protestant work ethic will feel right at home with the proverbs that encourage the character trait of *diligence*. Observing nature is one way to learn:

- "Go to the ant, you lazybones; consider its ways, and be wise. Without having any chief or officer or ruler, it prepares its food in summer, and gathers its sustenance in harvest. How long will you lie there, O lazybones? When will you rise from your sleep?" (Prov 6:6–9);

- Laziness is discouraged since it inevitably leads to poverty and hunger: "The lazy person does not plow in season; harvest comes, and there is nothing to be found" (Prov 20:4);

- "Laziness brings on deep sleep; an idle person will suffer hunger" (Prov 19:15).

- Readers recoil at the apt simile of Prov 10:26: "Like vinegar to the teeth, and smoke to the eyes, so are the lazy to their employers."

Honesty in speech, testimony, and trade is encouraged as the mark of the wise. Gossiping is to be avoided in favor of truth telling:

- "A gossip goes about telling secrets, but one who is trustworthy in spirit keeps a confidence" (Prov 11:13);

- "One who gives an honest answer gives a kiss on the lips" (Prov 24:26).

- Appropriate speech is praised with typical biblical enthusiasm:

- "A word fitly spoken is like apples of gold in a setting of silver" (Prov 25:11);

- "Pleasant words are like a honeycomb, sweetness to the soul and health to the body" (Prov 16:24);

- "A gentle tongue is a tree of life, but perverseness in it breaks the spirit" (Prov 15:4).

- We can all benefit from the proverbial wisdom, "Even fools who keep silent are considered wise; when they close their lips, they are deemed intelligent" (Prov 17:28).

Honesty in speech is especially important in judicial testimony. False witness is prohibited in the Ten Commandments, and Proverbs reiterates the prohibition:

- "A faithful witness does not lie, but a false witness breathes out lies" (Prov 14:5);

- "Lying lips are an abomination to the LORD, but those who act faithfully are his delight" (Prov 12:22).

- Deceitful trade practices are expressly forbidden: "Honest balances and scales are the LORD's; all the weights in the bag are his work" (Prov 16:11);

- "Bread gained by deceit is sweet, but afterward the mouth will be full of gravel" (Prov 20:17);

- "Those who are greedy for unjust gain make trouble for their households, but those who hate bribes will live" (Prov 15:27).

Positive character traits encouraged in Proverbs are *generosity and forgiveness*. In an agricultural subsistence economy, families depended on generosity and reciprocity to survive the hard times.

- "Those who are generous are blessed, for they share their bread with the poor" (Prov 22:9);

- "Whoever is kind to the poor lends to the LORD, and will be repaid in full" (Prov 19:17).

- Living in close community calls for generosity of spirit: "One who forgives an affront fosters friendship, but one who dwells on disputes will alienate a friend" (Prov 17:9).

- Further, generosity is to be enacted even with enemies: "If your enemies are hungry, give them bread to eat; and if they are thirsty, give them water to drink; for you will heap coals of fire on their heads, and the LORD will reward you" (Prov 25:21; see Rom 12:20).

- Many proverbial sayings encourage control of appetites in general, and particularly *control of anger*. "A fool gives full vent to anger, but the wise quietly holds it back" (Prov 29:11);

- "The beginning of strife is like letting out water; so stop before the quarrel breaks out" (Prov 17:14);

- "Those with good sense are slow to anger, and it is their glory to overlook an offense" (Prov 19:11).

- One way to control one's own anger is to choose associates carefully: "Make no friends with those given to anger, and do not associate with hotheads, or you may learn their ways and entangle yourself in a snare" (Prov 22:24).

- Once anger is uncontrolled, the results are entirely predictable: "For as pressing milk produces curds, and pressing the nose produces blood, so pressing anger produces strife" (Prov 30:33).

- Anger is to be avoided because, "Better is a dry morsel with quiet than a house full of feasting with strife" (Prov 17:1).

- We can understand the teachings of Proverbs as promoting *moderation*. "Do not be among winebibbers, or among gluttonous eaters of meat; for the drunkard and the glutton will come to poverty, and drowsiness will clothe them with rags" (Prov 23:20);

- "If you have found honey, eat only enough for you, or else, having too much, you will vomit it" (Prov 25:16);

- "Like a city breached, without walls, is one who lacks self-control" (Prov 25:28). In other words, "Good sense wins favor, but the way of the faithless is their ruin" (Prov 13:15).

THE CHARACTER OF GOD

It should be obvious by now that the biblical notion of character is dependent upon the character of God. The character traits encouraged in Israel are those traits found in the God of Israel. What do the biblical texts say about the character of God? Much could be said in answer to that question, but one particular passage is the paradigmatic description of God's character. Functioning as a creed for ancient Israel, the text appears eight times in the Old Testament, with only very slight variations. The first canonical presentation of the creedal statement is located after the golden-calf incident at Mount Sinai and solidifies God's recommitment to this people. Moses asks for a sign of God's presence, and God replies, "I will make all my goodness pass before you, and will proclaim before you the name, 'The LORD'; and I will be gracious to whom I will be gracious, and will show mercy on whom I will show mercy" (Exod 33:19). After Moses had cut the two new stone tablets and climbed Mount Sinai again, "The LORD passed before him [Moses], and proclaimed, 'The LORD, the LORD, a God merciful [*rachum*] and gracious [*chanan*], slow to anger, and abounding in steadfast love [*chesed*] and faithfulness [*'emet*], keeping steadfast love [*chesed*] for the thousandth generation, forgiving iniquity and transgression and sin, yet by no means clearing the guilty, but visiting the iniquity of the parents upon the children and the children's children, to the third and the fourth generation" (Exod 34:6–7; see also Num 14:18; Neh 9:17; Ps 86:15; 103:8; 145:8; Joel 2:13; Jonah 4:2). A brief look at the Hebrew reveals the depth God's passion for God's people.

The word *rachum*, translated "merciful" in the NRSV, is an adjective from the Hebrew root *r-ch-m*. The noun from this root is *rechem*, which means "womb." By now the reader will have noticed that Hebrew derives parts of speech from the same root letters, something that is hard to capture in an English translation. So, to take one example, a decisive decider decides a decision. In this case, we ask, If the noun from *r-ch-m* is "womb," what is the adjective? What adjective describes the feelings someone has for what is in her womb (or his wife's womb)? We don't have a single adjective in English to capture the breadth and depth of such feelings: protective, anxious, eager, excited, nurturing, maternal/paternal, or the like. Whatever feelings human parents have for their offspring, God has those feelings (and more) for Israel, since Israel is God's firstborn (see Exod 4:22). The first character trait mentioned for God seeks to capture the deep and abiding parental womb-feelings (*rachum*) that God has for Israel. Beyond that, God is *chanan*, "gracious." The verbal root *ch-n-n* means to give a gift to someone for no good reason, simply because one wants to give a gift; the noun, then, is "grace." Then the creed affirms God's long-suffering patience ("slow to anger"), a character trait confirmed by the seemingly endless chances given to God's people. Even when some part of the community bears the consequence of disobedience, God preserves a remnant to carry on as God's people.

The next section of the creed lists two character traits in which God abounds—*chesed* and *'emet*. *Chesed* is probably the quintessential example of a Hebrew word that has no good English equivalent. The NRSV translation chooses "steadfast love" most frequently but uses other words as well, depending on the context. From an analysis of English words, we can see three important characteristics of *chesed*. First, *chesed* points to favorable feelings toward another, reflected in words like "kindness," "faithful love," "mercy," "favor," and "devotion." Second, *chesed* signals a long-term relationship sustained over time, evident in words like "loyalty," "constancy," and "everlasting love." Third, *chesed* involves active engagement by the subject, manifest in phrases such as "good deeds" and "faithful deeds," and in words such as "clemency." That is, *chesed* is an action word, not just an emotion or feeling. Summarizing, *chesed* is a word that grows out of the committed covenant relationship that demonstrates favor toward the partner. Two uses of the translation "covenant loyalty" capture the aspects of long-lasting, active, favor: "Know therefore that the LORD your God is God, the faithful God who maintains covenant loyalty [*chesed*] with those who love him and keep his commandments, to a thousand generations," (Deut 7:9); "If you heed these ordinances, by diligently observing them, the LORD your God will maintain with you the covenant loyalty [*chesed*] that he swore to your ancestors" (Deut 7:12). The other facet of God's character that abounds is *'emet*, most often translated as "faithfulness." The Hebrew root *'-m-n* literally means "to lean on," so the characteristic being described is literally, "ability to be leaned on." The ancient testimony is that God is reliable, trustworthy, faithful, and dependable.

The second part of the ancient creed addresses God's justice with respect to declaring guilt and innocence. The primary testimony to God's character is that God forgives iniquity, transgression, and sin. Any reader of the Old Testament would find this description of God consistent with the repeated narratives of a "stiff-necked" people who continue to stray from the demands of the covenant. But the creed is quick to note that the guilty do not go scot-free; God does not completely acquit the guilty—that is, ignore the iniquity, transgression, or sin. There are consequences from sinful actions, which echo even into the third and fourth generations. While these consequences may be painful, the creed reassures all that God's *chesed* extends to the thousandth generation.

For Further Reading

READERS ARE URGED TO consult biblical commentaries and Bible dictionaries to explore citations and topics.

CHAPTER 1: CREATION

Anderson, Bernhard W. *From Creation to New Creation: Old Testament Perspectives.* Overtures to Biblical Theology. Minneapolis: Fortress, 1994.

———, editor. *Creation in the Old Testament.* Issues in Religion and Theology 6. Philadelphia: Fortress, 1984.

Brown, William P., and S. Dean McBride Jr., editors. *God Who Creates: Essays in Honor of W. Sibley Towner.* Grand Rapids: Eerdmans, 2000.

Clifford, Richard J. *Creation Accounts in the Ancient Near East and in the Bible.* Catholic Biblical Quarterly Monograph Series 26. Washington, DC: Catholic Biblical Association of America, 1994.

Fretheim, Terence E. *God and World in the Old Testament: A Relational Theology of Creation.* Nashville: Abingdon, 2005.

Levenson, Jon Douglas. *Creation and the Persistence of Evil: The Jewish Drama of Divine Omnipotence.* San Francisco: Harper & Row, 1988.

Simkins, Ronald A. *Creator & Creation: Nature in the Worldview of Ancient Israel.* Peabody, MA: Hendrickson, 1994.

CHAPTER 2: COVENANT

Levenson, Jon Douglas. *Sinai and Zion: An Entry into the Jewish Bible.* Minneapolis: Winston, 1985.

McCarthy, Dennis J. *Treaty and Covenant: A Study in Form in the Ancient Oriental Documents and in the Old Testament.* New ed. Analecta Biblica 21A. Rome: Pontifical Biblical Institute, 1978.

McKenzie, Steven L. *Covenant*. Understanding Biblical Themes. St. Louis: Chalice, 2000.

Niehaus, Jeffrey Jay. *God at Sinai: Covenant and Theophany in the Bible and the Ancient Near East*. Studies in Old Testament Biblical Theology. Grand Rapids: Zondervan, 1995.

Nicholson, Ernest W. *God and His People: Covenant and Theology in the Old Testament*. Oxford: Clarendon, 1986.

Sakenfeld, Katherine Doob. *Faithfulness in Action: Loyalty in Biblical Perspective*. Overtures to Biblical Theology 16. Minneapolis: Fortress, 1985.

Weinfeld, Moshe. *Social Justice in Ancient Israel and in the Ancient Near East*. Publications of the Perry Foundation for Biblical Research in the Hebrew University of Jerusalem. Minneapolis: Fortress, 1995.

CHAPTER 3: CULTUS

Ackerman, Susan. *Under Every Green Tree: Popular Religion in Sixth-Century Judah*. Harvard Semitic Monographs 46. Atlanta: Scholars, 1992.

Balentine, Samuel E. *The Torah's Vision of Worship*. Overtures to Biblical Theology. Minneapolis: Fortress, 1999.

Nelson, Richard D. *Raising Up a Faithful Priest: Community and Priesthood in Biblical Theology*. Louisville: Westminster John Knox, 1993.

Gammie, John G. *Holiness in Israel*. Overtures to Biblical Theology. Minneapolis: Fortress, 1989.

Miller, Patrick D. *The Religion of Ancient Israel*. Library of Ancient Israel. Louisville: Westminster John Knox, 2000.

Stevens, Marty E. *Temples, Tithes, and Taxes: The Temple and the Economic Life of Ancient Israel*. Peabody, PA: Hendrickson, 2006.

Vaux, Roland de. *Ancient Israel: Its Life and Institutions*. New York: McGraw-Hill, 1961.

CHAPTER 4: CHARACTER

Barton, John. *Ethics and the Old Testament*. London: SCM, 1998.

Birch, Bruce C. *Let Justice Roll Down: The Old Testament, Ethics, and Christian Life*. Louisville: Westminster John Knox, 1991.

Brown, William P. *The Ethos of the Cosmos: The Genesis of Moral Imagination in the Bible*. Grand Rapids: Eerdmans, 1999.

———, editor. *Character and Scripture: Moral Formation, Community and Biblical Interpretation.* Grand Rapids: Eerdmans, 2002.

Stevens, Marty E. "The Obedience of Trust: Recovering the Law as Gift." In *The Ten Commandments: The Reciprocity of Faithfulness*, edited by William P. Brown, 133–45. Library of Theological Ethics. Louisville: Westminster John Knox, 2000.

Scripture Index